McGuffey

Other books by Etta B. Degering:
Little Lad
Little Maid
My Bible Friends (books 1-5)
My Friend Jesus

To order, call 1-800-765-6955.

Visit us at **www.AutumnHousePublishing.com**
for information on other Autumn House® products.

McGuffey

The
GREATEST
FORGOTTEN MAN

Etta B. Degering

Autumn
House® Publishing
www.autumnhousepublishing.com
A Division of **REVIEW AND HERALD® PUBLISHING**
Since 1861

Copyright © 2011 by Review and Herald® Publishing Association

Published by Autumn House® Publishing, a division of Review and Herald® Publishing, Hagerstown, MD 21741-1119

All rights reserved. No portion of this book may be reproduced, stored in a retrieval system, or transmitted in any form or by any means (electronic, mechanical, photocopy, recording, scanning, or other), except for brief quotations in critical reviews or articles, without the prior written permission of the publisher.

Autumn House® titles may be purchased in bulk for educational, business, fund-raising, or sales promotional use. For information, please e-mail SpecialMarkets@reviewandherald.com.

Autumn House® Publishing publishes biblically based materials for spiritual, physical, and mental growth and Christian discipleship.

The author assumes full responsibility for the accuracy of all facts and quotations as cited in this book.

This book was
Edited by Penny Estes Wheeler
Designed by Trent Truman
Cover art by © istockphoto.com / Goldmund
Typeset: Goudy 11/14

PRINTED IN U.S.A.

15 14 13 12 11   5 4 3 2 1

Library of Congress Cataloging-in-Publication Data

Degering, Etta.
  McGuffey : the greatest forgotten man / Etta B. Degering.
      p. cm.
  Includes bibliographical references and index.
1. McGuffey, William Holmes, 1800-1873. 2. Educators—United States—History. 3. Moral education—United States—History. 4. Readers—History. I. Title.
LA2317.M2D44 2011
370.92—dc22
[B]
                              2010017620

ISBN 978-0-8127-0502-7

To Trudy Anne,
the teacher in our family

ACKNOWLEDGMENTS

This book has been made possible by the generous help of many people. Their willingness to assist suggests the esteem with which they evaluate the contribution William Holmes McGuffey made to American heritage. I cannot mention all, but wish at least to record those who helped in a special way.

First on my list are Miss Charlotte Leonard, coordinator of children's services in Montgomery County, Ohio, and her group of librarians who suggested their library shelves were awaiting a biography of William Holmes McGuffey. Thank you, Miss Leonard and Montgomery County librarians, for the suggestion.

Mrs. Clara Belle Thomas and Mary McGuffey Speer, grand-nieces of William McGuffey residing in New Wilmington, Pennsylvania, contributed the framework of genealogy that kept the biography evolving in chronological sequence.

Mr. and Mrs. Thomas E. Rogers (Mrs. Rogers is a great, great grandniece of McGuffey) entertained my husband and me one snowy afternoon in Youngstown, Ohio, recounting by picture and story the former and recent history of Gravel Hill, the old McGuffey homestead. The "recent" included the ceremonial placing of a historical marker by state and national officials to mark the site. We drove along the McGuffey Road and tried to imagine the giant

trees that William as a boy helped his father cut down when building the road from the homestead to Youngstown. The giants have
given way to cornfields or stands of lesser timber. The lake at
Gravel Hill has disappeared. The only evidence of the original
homesteaders is the well atop the hill. But we were told a complete
restoration is in the offing. May it succeed.

Dr. Hardigg Sexton, host at the McGuffey Museum, and Steven
Millett, assistant host, demonstrated the "second mile" of courtesy
during my research in Oxford, Ohio. The museum, occupying the
red (now white) brick house that William McGuffey built on
Spring Street, includes in its exhibits the octagonal table on which
he compiled the four little books that made him famous, Harriet
McGuffey's portrait which plays a nostalgic part in the story, the
teacher's contract signed by 14-year-old William, the largest col-
lection extant of McGuffey Readers, the black horsehair sofa, and
many other items of interesting memorabilia. My less esthetic curiosity found satisfaction on seeing the bust of McGuffey, not because of its artistic execution but because of a family incident when
two little girls placed the bust of their father in the bed of a certain
Miss Sarah. In the museum's archives one may read Henrietta
McGuffey's eight-volume, hand-written reminiscences of family
life, McGuffey's hand-written philosophy text, and numerous
other related manuscripts and documents—an encyclopedic treas-
ury to the researcher.

Of great importance in my quest for McGuffey anecdote was the
folder of more than 200 letters that Dr. John Weatherby, assistant
librarian of Miami University, Oxford, Ohio, handed me across
his desk with the comment, "You'll want to see these." I surely did.
The collection consists of letters written to and by Wm. H.
McGuffey, as he usually signed his name. Other letters proved to
be testimonials of those who had personally known him.

I wish also to express my appreciation for the contribution
made by two other Oxford citizens: Dr. William E. Smith,

ex-curator of the McGuffey Museum and Mrs. William Orne Cullen, Jr., of the Cullen Printing Company, Oxford, who gave permission to make copies of the pictures in Dr. Smith's copyrighted booklet, *About the McGuffeys*.

Mrs. James Saxon, reference librarian of the Washington and Jefferson College, Washington, Pennsylvania, contributed the photostat of the hand-copied page from the Hebrew grammar which William McGuffey, when a student at the college, copied with quill and ink because he could not afford to buy the textbook.

Librarian Geraldine Hope of Archives, Ohio University at Athens, Ohio, furnished the account of the McGuffey Elms, also other information in the form of unpublished manuscripts.

Reference librarian Kendon L. Stubba of the University of Virginia, Charlottesville, Virginia, directed my research at that institution which included letters and manuscripts concerning the McGuffeys during the Civil War, also episodes connected with the McGuffey Ash. I visited the oval east room (McGuffey's classroom in the Rotunda), took pictures of the Ash, his grave, and Pavilion Number 9 where he lived the last 28 years of his life. If only brick and mortar could speak!

I would not forget the help of librarians in my own Mile High Country: the Denver and Boulder public libraries, the University of Colorado. No book could be written without the help of librarians. My thank you to them, one and all.

CONTENTS

Born in 1800, William McGuffey's childhood on the Ohio frontier was so different from life today that it is hard to even imagine it. Take away our e-mail and Internet, land phones and electricity, glass windows, carpet, and cars, even pencils and paper—and we still will have little conception of what life in an unheated log cabin was like 200 years ago.

This fact is reflected in how different their vocabulary of everyday things was from words commonly used today. For that reason I compiled a list of words unfamiliar to me, thinking that they might be new for you too. When the word had more than one definition, I chose the one closest to how it is used in this book.

—the editor

VOCABULARY
OF THE 1800S

Belles-Lettres: from the French for literature, literally "fine letters"; literature that is appreciated for the beauty, artistry, and originality of style and tone rather than for its ideas and content

bombazine: a silk fabric, twill weave, dyed black

cambric: thin fine white linen

cat-and-clay chimney: chimney formed with sticks but covered with clay (usually mixed with straw or grass for added strength) which has been applied three-inches-thick both inside and out

dirk: a dagger

fisticuffs: a fistfight

girding: cutting a deep circle around a tree trunk so that the tree will die

grandees: persons of elevated rank or station

helve: handle of the ax or of a weapon

hewed: shaped with heavy cutting blows

hip roof: a roof with sloping ends and sloping sides

impressment: seizing individuals and forcing them into service

lee: the side sheltered from the wind

lessee: a person who has leased property and is paying rent on it

linsey-woolsey: a coarse heavy fabric woven from wool and linen or cotton

mast: foods, such as acorns, on a forest floor serving as food for birds and animals

maul: heavy hammer with a wooden head, especially used to drive wedges

peltry: the sale of skins, usually untreated, of small animals

piggin: a small wooden pail; one slat extended up above the pail as a handle

puncheon: a split log with the face smoothed

puncheon floor: a floor made of split logs, usually of poplar or ash, the flat side smoothed with a broad-ax

quirt: a shirt-handled riding whip

registrant: a person who has registered

scrip: a document showing that the holder is entitled to something, usually money; paper currency or token used in an emergency

slewed: to turn or twist

spring beauty: the purslane family; usually has a two-leaf stem and pink flower

The year without a summer: the result of the April 15, 1815, eruption of Mount Tambora on the Indonesian island of Sumbawa—one of the largest eruptions of modern history. It blocked out solar radiation, causing, in 1816, an extremely cold spring and summer in Europe and the United States, and much hardship.

tow cloth: coarse cloth woven from the hemp plant; used by the poorest of the poor

withes: slender, flexible branches or twigs

wooden trenchers: a platter for eating or serving food

INTRODUCTION:
WHO WAS MCGUFFEY?

Ask a boy of the one-room log or the little red schoolhouse. If teacher's back were turned, his freckled face most likely would break into a grin as he answered, Old Second Reader.

Ask a homespun-clad student who had walked 50 miles through virgin forest to attend Ohio Miami University. His drawling reply: "Guff? He be professor o'Mental and Moral Philosophy."

Ask the Press of the early nineteen hundreds: "The man who wrote five little books that helped mold a Nation . . . who delivered childhood from *Wigglesworth's Day of Do* and brought a renaissance to the schoolroom."

Ask the same source less than a quarter century later. In bold headlines comes the reply: "McGUFFEY IS THE GREATEST FORGOTTEN MAN."

Scotch-Irish by ancestry, Pennsylvanian by birth, William McGuffey grew up on the Ohio frontier as the echo of Indian war whoops faded into the west. It is said he could sling an ax, memorize a chapter of the Bible, or a chapter of history with equal ease. In later life he became an adopted Virginian.

Roving teacher days revealed to him the dire need of a series of readers slanted toward cosmopolitan America settling the country between the Appalachian and Rocky Mountains. With no thought of fame he authored four little readers and collaborated with his brother on a fifth. The readers led boys and girls from "A is for ax," the implement that changed the West, through a story

15

land both real and fabled, to the best in classical prose and poetry—each selection defining a principle of good citizenship.

In a single generation McGuffey, by means of five little books, welded the diverse cultures and languages of the nationalities pushing west—German, Swedish, Norwegian, Scotch-Irish—into a unified American society. The Readers have been acclaimed the most influential volumes of America in molding the nation's thought during the more than half a century from Martin Van Buren to Theodore Roosevelt. Materially, they were responsible for an obscure Cincinnati firm becoming the largest textbook publishers in America. The books made 10 millionaires, their author not included.

The purpose of this book is to tell the story of the man behind the readers, to answer the question: Who was McGuffey?

CHAPTER ONE

On The Northwest Trail

Mid-May, 1803, brought the dogwoods of western Pennsylvania into full bloom. White clumps frosted hillsides and outlined swollen creeks. They brightened the undergrowth of the hardwood forest through which the old Indian trail led northwest from Fort Pitt on the headwaters of the Ohio to the village of Youngstown on the Mahoning River in the brand new state of Ohio. The trail had originally been plowed by the hooves of buffalo and tramped firm by the moccasin-clad feet of native Americans. Both had now pushed, or been pushed, westward beyond the sound of the White man's ax and adz, beyond his steel-pointed plow that furrowed centuries-old feeding and hunting grounds.

On the trail this May day a tall solidly-built man, measuring distance with a woodsman's stride, led a pair of packhorses single file. The horses, one black, the other white, carried his family (wife and three small children), rolls of blankets, and saddlebags bulging with household goods. Lead rope always taut, the man pulled the caravan along with an enthusiasm which in turn seemed to be pulling him, an enthusiasm known in the land rush of 1803 as Ohio Fever.

The man was an ex-Indian scout, Scotch-Irish Alexander McGuffey, "Sandy" to his friends. When the territory south of lake Erie opened for settlement after the Indian wars, Sandy McGuffey had returned to the scene of his scouting days to purchase a tract of timberland near Youngstown. He knew the tract well, even to the smell of its loam, having crawled through a part of it on hands and knees. He acquired the 165-acre claim for $500 on a long-term payment plan and immediately began improvements. He deadened a small plot of woods for corn by girding the trees while still in full leaf, grubbed out the underbrush, cut logs and built a cabin, then returned to Washington County, Pennsylvania for his family. Warned every mile of the journey back to the claim that corn-planting time had come—"Plant corn when the dogwoods have come into full bloom," advised the farmers' almanac—Sandy urged the horses to a faster pace.

On the broad back of the white mare equipped with packsaddle, rode Anna Holmes McGuffey holding her youngest, baby Henry Holmes. Ahead of her in baskets of hickory withes, slung from either side of the black horse led by Sandy, rode the two older children, 4-year-old talkative Jane and 2 ½-year-old William Holmes, sober as an Indian papoose. Anna had slipped her maiden name, Holmes, into each of her sons' names. "I have to lay some claim to them," she laughingly told friends, "since they both take after their father." Both boys had the high McGuffey forehead, sky-blue eyes, wide mouths, and noses already budding into prominence. The one difference between Sandy and sons, other than size, was color of their hair. Henry's tended toward red, William's toward black, instead of the flaxen mop that earned Sandy his nickname.

A whimpering brown puppy, hovered over by the solicitous Jane, occupied a smaller basket between the children. "Curly wants his ma," William told his sister. Anna smiled. The boy ought to know. Not too long ago he had whimpered for a similar reason. He had protested against giving up his place in her arms and his cradle beside her bed, to the new baby brother.

To a knowing observer, the cut of Anna's blue linsey-woolsey dress, the pert style of her ribbon bonnet, and her way of speaking suggested an upbringing culturally above that of the average woodsman's wife—a background of plenty with fair schooling. Yet one noticed that at times something seemed to be troubling her, especially when her attention focused on the boys. Then her forehead creased into a frown as if some problem rode along the trail with her, a problem she could not solve.

The frown quickly vanished if Sandy turned to point out some interesting bit of woods lore: rumpled ground under a buckeye tree that had been raked by the toes of hundreds of carrier pigeons searching for mast—much mast, many wild pigeons; a mockingbird on the topmost branch of a hickory singing a medley of other birds' songs; the girth of an oak that would probably show 300 growth rings if logged. Then Anna's face lit with admiration. Sandy knew his forest, knew it from mast to mocker to the age of oaks.

At times the trail sliced a thin line through the forest, the ribbon of sky showing deep blue. But most of the way it burrowed a tunnel through dappled shade, the trees interlacing branches overhead, their roots making corduroy of the path underfoot. The horses sometimes stumbled over the rib-like roots, causing packs to shift.

"Is the trail like this all the way?" Anna asked during a halt to adjust saddlebags. "Does it never come out in the open? I'd like to see what's beyond the trees."

Sandy laughed. "You'd see more trees. I once heard an old hunter say, 'A man can travel in the shade, if he's a-mind to, the hull way from the Ohio to the Great Lakes 'cept when crossin' streams."

"Aren't you tired, Sandy?"

"Tired? Truth, lass, I'm not even warmed up yet."

Packs adjusted, Sandy snatched a handful of spring beauties for each cramped basket rider to "pretty the horse's mane."

Again taking the lead rope, he resumed the long swinging stride that showed no fatigue.

Sandy's buoyant eagerness belied his 35 years, reminding Anna of the first time she ever saw him. He was then a rangy young fellow not long out of his teens. The McGuffeys had just moved from New York State, where they had lived since migrating from Scotland when Sandy was 5, to Wheeling Creek about two miles from Rural Grove, her father's homestead. Rural Grove! A wave of homesickness spread through her as she pictured its 400 acres, its two-story house, the only two-story log house in Washington County. Would she ever see it again?

Sandy had come to Rural Grove one evening to deliver a pair of shoes his father, William McGuffey (little William was named for him) had made for her father. The senior McGuffey preferred farming but cobbled shoes on the side for ready cash, and fine shoes they were. Errand accomplished, Sandy had jubilantly announced that he was joining the American forces operating out of Fort Washington (Cincinnati) as an Indian scout.

No, his pa wasn't exactly pleased about his going, he admitted. Fact was, he wanted him to study books. Sandy had glanced at the six books on the Holmes's mantel and shrugged. "Guess I just don't take to book larnin'," he'd added.

Then shaking hands good-bye with Father and Mother Holmes, he had gone whistling down the lane, dog Jock, a black and white mongrel with plumed tail, at his heels. He had not so much thrown a glance Anna's way, for she had been a pigtailed, pinafored 13 at the time

Anna looked at the height and breadth of the man bending to the trail ahead (there was no Jock now, but she wouldn't think of that) and wondered how he had managed to conceal such a frame from Indian counterspies. She shuddered as she remembered the tales of daring and narrow escape that had filtered back to Rural Grove during the years of his scouting—from General

St. Clair's defeat to Anthony Wayne's victory. There was the time he lay all day in a swamp counting the strength of painted warriors amassing to fight the Whites; the time he ran 41 miles in the dark of night to warn his superior of danger; the time he outwitted Red pursuers with an empty gun. And then the Indian wars were over. Defeated, the Native Americans had pushed westward, and Sandy had come home for good.

Shortly after his return he had visited Rural Grove on some errand; she didn't remember what. But she would never forget his look of surprise when she opened the door, and how he all but forgot the purpose of his visit. She was now 19. Her pigtails had become ringlets piled high; the pinafore, a slim-bodiced, full-skirted frock. After that day, errands between Wheeling Creek and Rural Grove multiplied. Did Sandy really think she hadn't guessed his purpose behind those errands? Men might fool Indians, but maidens—never!

Other suitors had sought her hand, among them the village schoolmaster, but Sandy had been persistent. And so at high noon on Christmas day, 1797, they were married in the parlor at Rural Grove. Neighbors, friends, and relatives came from miles around to make merry and to enjoy the two wedding feasts, one at the McGuffey's, the other at her home. Midnight brought the festivities to a close with Sandy carrying her upstairs to the rooms where they then lived more than five years, where Jane, William, and Henry had been . . .

With a start Anna realized the horses had come to a halt beside a creek and Sandy was speaking to her. "Might we should eat our lunch here," he suggested, squinting at the sky as a man accustomed to telling time by the sun.

The children, joyous at being released from the confining baskets, ran hither and yon, Jane leading, William next, and the puppy, upended as often as right side up, trying to follow. Baby Henry, propped against a tree trunk, crowed at the antics of sister and brother. Anna seated her family on a log for lunch and handed out thick meat sandwiches and ginger cookies as large as saucers. No time to loiter, they were soon on their way again.

Late afternoon brought them to a sweet-water spring, their goal for the night. Even Sandy admitted he had had a day. He swung the packs down from the drooping horses, hobbled them, gave each a "well-done" slap, and turned them loose to graze along the spring runoff. Anna put a kettle to boil over a fire that Sandy built between the blackened stones left by some former camper, and prepared a supper of cornmeal porridge. After supper they all gathered leaves for a mattress, adding them to those lately shed by a spreading oak. Jane tossed her leaves with abandon, William placed his with precision. Blankets spread on top the leaves completed the bed.

Hardly had dusk descended when the family lay down to sleep. Sandy, rifle at hand, slept as soon as he touched the blanket; the children, even the puppy in Jane's arms, soon after. But sleep was a long time coming to Anna. A wolf howled in the distance; Sandy stirred, turned over. An owl *who-o-o-ed* from the top of a white oak stump. But it was neither the wolf nor the owl that kept Anna awake. As darkness closed in about her so did the problem that had plagued her on the trail. The problem concerned her boys. Sandy was a woodsman through and through. That he looked forward to William and Henry and any other boys they might have growing up as woodsmen was only natural. He saw no need for "book larnin'" beyond the simplest ciphering, reading, and writing. But she was determined—and her determination made her feel a twinge of guilt and disloyalty toward Sandy—that the boys should have an education, a college education. After that, if they chose to be woodsmen instead of following a profession, well and good. But they should have a chance to choose.

Secretly she hoped one of the boys would choose to be a minister. Not a circuit-riding backwoods preacher (God forgive if she were being uppity), but an ordained minister who could read the Bible in the language it was written. She thought it was Hebrew, or was it Greek? And if one boy looked after people's souls perhaps the other could look after their bodies—be a doctor. And should there be another boy, law was an honorable calling.

But where and how could they get a training for such? On the frontier where they were going, there wasn't even a church let alone a school of higher learning. Every mile of the trail took her boys a mile farther away from a proper education.

Anna felt the saddlebag alongside of where she lay. The books were there—a *Noah Webster's Blue-backed Speller* and the family Bible. She would teach all of her children to read and write, girls as well as boys, though the only future for girls was marriage, of course. With boys it was different. They could become whatever they set their minds to if only they could get the proper book learning. She sighed. She could see no future for William and Henry beyond the *Blue-backed Speller*.

Maybe it was the star-pricked heavens glimpsed through the oak's branches, or the stillness of the forest, or her early training that spoke to her. Whichever it was, perhaps all three, she began to chide herself for lack of faith. Hadn't both she and Sandy been brought up strict Presbyterian Covenanters? And didn't Covenanters believe that Providence overrules in the affairs of men if they but trust Him? Why then should she try to assume the whole burden? She resolved to trust. Somewhere, somehow, her boys would receive a proper education. With the resolve to trust came sleep.

Sixty-five miles out from Fort Pitt the trail climbed a ridge that looked down on the valley through which flowed the Mahoning River. A blue haze of smoke, rising from smoldering stumps in clearings, lay over it all. Anna counted 12 or 15 weathered log cabins huddled together on the east bank of the river below the junction of a creek. This was Youngstown, and it was now her town.

Sandy halted the caravan, looped the lead rope over the black horse's mane, and stepped back beside her to enumerate the advantages the town offered. He pointed to the new gristmill being built on the falls of the creek where they would get their corn ground into meal; no 40- or 80-mile trek to a mill as many a settler on the frontier had to make. The largest of the cabins, the one next to the river, he explained, was the district trading post where produce could be bartered for trade goods and where the overland post carrier deposited and picked up mail every fortnight. And already the town had a physician in residence. Eyes twinkled as he added, "I heard tell before leaving, that a parson-schoolmaster, name of Wick, is holding both church and school in his cabin."

One more thing he wanted her to see—north of the town on a slope in the hazy distance was a treeless plot toward which trails from every direction converged. "The trails lead to a salt spring," he said, "where all the salt we'll need to preserve our meat can be had for the boiling."

In early afternoon the McGuffeys began the last lap of their journey, the five and-a-half miles east and north of Youngstown to Sandy's claim at Gravel Hill. A surveyor had told Sandy that the crested ridge in the otherwise flat-like terrain had been deposited by a glacier in the long ago. But a recent use had given the hill its gritty name. Someone had dug gravel from its side, and ever since it had been called Gravel Hill.

Anna turned in her saddle to have a last look at the cabin where she and her family had been so hospitably entertained during the recent passing of a thundershower. She knew it would be months before she again saw smoke feathering up from a chimney other than her own. Cabin and smoke were blotted from view when the horses entered a beech woods where dense branches continued the shower and silvery trunks challenged their right of way. Here, no buffalo had plowed out a trace; perhaps the shaggy beasts had read the beeches' no trespassing sign. Sandy whistled as he forged ahead, or backtracked, searching for a passage wide enough for the pack animals, getting his general direction from a creek bed known as Dry Run, but which was anything but dry after the thundershower.

"Trees are a clue to the soil," he told Anna. "Beeches grow only in the best, and the richer the soil the bigger they grow. Someday we'll have us a road through this woods right to our clearing."

The beeches towering above Sandy dwarfed him to a child. Yet he spoke with confidence of a road and a clearing, knowing full well that such an undertaking meant pitting his personal strength and a four-inch ax blade against an entire forest. How many years, Anna wondered, would pass before "someday" arrived.

The forest welcomed them with a spring show. Redbuds, dogwoods, and wild crabapples did their best with bloom and perfume; jack-in-the-pulpits pushed through brown turf; may apples raised leafy umbrellas over white flowers. At last the caravan rounded the base of Gravel Hill and the family had its first glimpse of their frontier home. Nestled in the lee of the hill with a lake forming the background to the left, stood a one-room, windowless, unchinked log cabin with hip roof and cats-and-clay chimney.

Sandy tied the horses to a tree beside the cabin stoop and took the sleeping Henry while Anna dismounted. Then he lifted William and Jane from their baskets and flung open the cabin door. The smell of new wood and musty earth rushed out to meet them.

As Anna's eyes became accustomed to the dim interior, lighted only by the open door and cracks between the logs, she saw an earth-packed floor, a fireplace in which Sandy had laid logs and kindling for their homecoming, and a table and benches that showed the marks of his adz. In a corner stood a bed. It had been made by driving notched poles into the earthen floor. From these poles other poles were cleated to the logs of the cabin walls. She turned from the pole bed, closing her mind against the memory of Rural Grove's canopy-frilled poster beds, to the cradle which Sandy had hollowed from a length of poplar. Placing a folded blanket in the cradle, she lay the sleeping Henry in his bed. Then she joined the family for the lighting of the hearth which initiates a home. Sandy had taken the flint from his gun and was kneeling before the fireplace. Jane and William knelt one on either side of him. With an ease born of experience Sandy struck the flint against the steel gun barrel, producing sparks which caught in the dry moss. Yellow flames licked at the pithy kindling and soon the heated logs began to sizzle and snap. Suddenly from between the logs a snake's head appeared, followed by a long black body that slithered to the floor. A lizard with singed tail followed the snake and ran wildly about the room.

Laughing uproariously, Sandy guided the trespassers toward the door. "I reckon the varmints found squatters rights a wee might too warm."

The children followed the creatures' exit, Jane squealing, William soberly watching every move. Anna snatched the baby from the cradle and froze, eyes fixed on the fireplace. What reptile would it produce next? She took a deep breath as homesickness engulfed her. Never . . . *never* had she seen a snake or lizard in the house at Rural Grove!

CHAPTER TWO

At Gravel Hill

Was it possible that three years had gone by since the day the pack horses halted before the cabin on the slope of Gravel Hill? Yes, it was true. If nothing else, the family itself confirmed the fact. The basket riders had grown out of the basket age. Jane was now 7, William nearing 6, and Henry, his red hair even redder, had turned 4. A new toddler, little Anna, raced with herself back and forth across the one-room cabin.

The years, for the most part, had been measured by the *thud, thud, thud* of Sandy's ax and adz. The clearing had been extended, the road to Youngstown well begun, a barn and granary built, and a well dug. The cabin walls had been chinked and re-chinked, a window cut into a wall, and a puncheon floor laid. When Sandy drove the last peg in the puncheon he assured Anna that the cabin was tight sealed against any straying varmints. "But what's so scary, lass, about a harmless old black snake or scampery little lizard?" he asked. "More than once I've waked in the woods to find I'd shared my bed with one or the other."

But harmless or little, scampery or slow, Anna had no intention of sharing her home with the creepy, crawling creatures of the forest.

Like the ticking of a clock, the thudding of Sandy's ax went unnoticed unless it stopped, which it did for a period each year. Those were the times that he tied ax, cooking pot, powder, and lead to the black horse's saddle, and leading the white mare took to the forest or swamp for a season of hunting or trapping. Land payments must be met, and peltry was the answer. During the days that followed his going, Anna often caught herself listening for the ax's familiar thud. The children, too, were restless. They missed Pa. They missed the sound of his ax that had become as much a part of their days as sunrise and sunset. Sandy's return set everything right. As a poet might say, "The ax thuds again. All is well."

Like most frontier women, Anna worked from before dawn until after dark. She worked too hard, Sandy said. But what else could a woman do when everything from soap to tallow dips, from the tanning of leather to the weaving of linsey-woolsey for clothes, from the churning of butter to salting down meat, as well as teaching the children to read and write depended on her. Sometimes, she admitted, she felt starved for the sight of another woman and for woman-talk. A man rode off to the mill or salt springs but a woman stayed by the cabin and the *bairns*. All this would be changed, Anna told herself, when the road was finished. Then the whole family could go by wagon to the Reverend Wick's for church, and the older children could walk to his school. So much depended on the road, and progress was painstakingly slow. Wood chip by wood chip by wood chip . . . by wood chip it inched its way toward Youngstown. Sandy worked at felling the trees in the evenings after he had worked all day in the clearing. And once the trees lay across the ground, the work had hardly begun.

Nor were the children idle. During the spring and summer Jane, William, and Henry got up with the sun. Besides fetching the wood and water and rounding up the cow at milking time, their special task, with the help of Curly, was keeping the squirrels out of the corn. And squirrels did not stay abed after sunup.

The last of May or first of June the corn, which had been planted Indian fashion with a hoe between the deadened trees, began to send up green points through black humus. Immediately the news spread from tree to tree in the forest, and hordes of squirrels converged on the sprouting corn. To a squirrel each spear of green marked the place of a juicy kernel that could be had for the digging. Gray squirrels, red squirrels, fox squirrels, black squirrels, albino squirrels, and squirrels with striped backs laid siege. An estimated billion squirrels overran the new state of Ohio, and sometimes the children thought most of them lived in their neighborhood.

Jane, William, and Henry shouted and shooed. They threw clods and stones. They beat tin pans with sticks, but Curly proved to be the champion squirrel chaser. Four legs were faster than two and fanged jaws deadlier than hastily thrown stones. And at night Curly guarded the corn against raccoons and warned humans if a bear climbed the brush fence.

Sometimes while Curly kept the scolding squirrels treed, the children snatched a few minutes of play. Jane and Henry built log houses with last year's corncobs, but William preferred to build words. Using the pointed end of a stick he wrote t-h-o-r-n on a smoothed place in the path. September last, on his fifth birthday, his mother had brought out the *Blue-backed Speller* and taught him and Jane their ABC's and how to spell one-syllable words. Each evening since then, the two oldest children spent some time writing and spelling. Hand-hewn ash slabs served as their slates and charcoal sticks as their pencils, and Ma was a particular teacher. Once she made William rewrite a whole slab full of words because he forgot to cross a T.

Some days William wrote families of words: cat, mat, hat, rat, sat, or fun, run, sun . . . But he liked best to try long hard ones like Cincinnati. Syllable by syllable, he sounded out the name:

29

"Sin-sin-at-e." Ma said it wasn't the way grownups spelled it, but anyway it read right.

Jane left the building of log houses to admire William's words. "However do you do it, William? How do you figure them out?"

William shrugged. "I—I just think."

"Ma says you've got a bent towards books, but Pa holds that book larnin' n'er yet helped a man cut down a tree." Jane studied the forest crowding the corn patch. "I reckon tree-cuttin' . . ."

"Cutting," William interrupted. "Ma says cuttin' is back-woods talk."

"I reckon tree cutting," Jane repeated, "is pretty important else the corn patch would always be smallish-like."

A flash of blue streaked by. "William, I do believe the blue-birds have got babies! They've been going in and out of their nest all morning."

In the newest deadening of the cornfield, a pair of bluebirds had built their nest in the hollow limb of a maple. How long they had used the maple for their home site no one knew. This year they had returned from the South as usual, before the trees leafed out, and renewed their nest. Jane feared that the bluebirds might leave when the deadened tree failed to furnish a leafy cover from enemies, especially when she and her brothers made such a racket chasing squirrels, but so far they had stayed. Old Blue, as they called the male, seemed unafraid and watched with interest the noisy goings-on from his high perch in the tree. Perhaps he actually gloried in seeing his enemy, the nest-robbing squirrels, bested. Now that the birds had a family they were sure to stay.

In a few weeks the corn had grown tough woody stalks and the squirrels lost interest in it, at least for a time. So the children turned to other tasks. William helped his father pile brush to fence a new deadening and he helped him sharpen his ax on the grindstone. The grindstone was set in a frame and turned by foot pedals. William's part was to hold a gourd of water above the revolving stone, letting the water dribble a steady flow, not too much, not too little, on the place of contact between stone and ax. He liked the slurpy, gritty sound and the sour, gray smell of grinding steel. Curly took an interest in the ax grinding too. It meant the man master would soon be leaving for the forest, and if the boy master went along, he, too, would get to go. The man took no notice of a dog's asking eyes or wagging tail, but the boy always whistled an invitation.

William puzzled over his father's attitude toward Curly. One day after the ax grinding, as he watched his father's retreating back and saw the dog's disappointment, he decided to ask his mother about it. He found her sitting on the bench under the silver maple at the end of the yard nearest the new road, knitting socks. (Both the tree and the bench had been Sandy's idea to enable Anna to get a little more rest.) He pulled himself up onto the bench beside her. Curly crawled under the bench but enough of him stretched beyond it to make a hairy footstool for a boy's bare feet. "Ma, why doesn't Pa ever take Curly with him?" William asked. "He never takes him anywhere."

Anna purled two, knitted two, completing the cuff of the sock, then carefully tucked the knitting into her work basket. "You know, son, that Curly's first duty is guarding the cabin, and he couldn't very well guard it if he were off somewhere in the woods." She looked away in the direction of the thudding ax, and added as if talking to herself, "But t'would be the same if we had any number of dogs."

Anna took a hank of wool from the basket—she didn't believe in wasting anything, time most of all—and held it toward William. "If you'll hold this wool while I wind it into a ball, I'll tell you a story. Then maybe you'll understand some things better."

William held out his arms. Anna looped the wool over them and began the ball. "When your pa was a boy in his teens, he had a dog named Jock. Jock was a short-legged black-and-white dog

31

with a bushy tail that curled like a skunk's tail over his back."

"Did you ever see Jock, Ma?"

"Yes, I saw Jock a number of times. He followed Sandy—that was before he was your pa—like a shadow, only not like a shadow either because a shadow follows only if the sun shines, and Jock was at Sandy's heels all the time. The two of them camped out for months at a time in the forest. Then came the Indian wars and Sandy joined the American army as a scout. He took Jock with him. He taught the dog to slip through the woods as silently as a fox, and never to bark, but point instead. If Sandy ran, Jock ran. If Sandy walked, Jock walked. If Sandy crawled, Jock crawled along beside him."

"Do you reckon we could teach Curly to be a scout?"

"I reckon so. Curly's a smart dog. His mother was watchdog at Rural Grove. But we'll hope there's no more need for Indian scouts."

"What happened to Jock, Ma? Did the Indians get him?"

Anna sighed. "No, the Indian's didn't get him. When Sandy and his buddy, Duncan McArthur, were sent north with Captain Brady to spy out the strength of the Indians dancing the war dance—your pa has told you that Indians always dance the war dance about their campfires before attacking—well, Jock as usual went along. Suddenly the men found themselves surrounded with painted warriors. They had to crawl from bush to bush. By daytime they kept their direction by the moss on trees, and nighttime by looking at the stars. They had nothing to eat but a few wild berries.

"After three days the captain became so weak he could go no farther without food. He said it was better that the dog die rather than the men, and ordered it so. Sandy crawled slowly away into the brush, Jock beside him. And when he crawled back to the men, he carried the lifeless body of his dog. So maybe now you can understand why your pa cannot bear to have another dog along with him."

William swallowed hard. His toes combed Curly's back. Curly gave the caressing feet a slobbery lick and his tail thumped the ground.

A breeze stirred the silver maple's leaves. Anna drew in quick little sniffs testing it. "I do believe the corn's starting to tassel. Nothing else has that same musky smell. And if I can smell it, so can the squirrels."

At the word squirrels, Curly sprang out from under the bench. Stiff-legged, ears erect, nose pointed toward the corn patch, he growled a warning.

Anna laughed. "From now until fall, old fellow, you and William will be kept busy."

And so it was. Corn tassels served as flag signals semaphoring far and wide that the corn had formed ears. The one kernel of corn, planted in the spring, had now produced one and sometimes two full ears of corn. The squirrels attacked in like proportion. No time now for building words or corncob cabins. Whooping like Indians on the warpath, the children chased squirrels all day long. At times even Anna had to help. And even quiet Old Blue, whose mate was sitting on a second clutch of eggs, joined the defending forces led by Curly. When a squirrel came too near his maple, he darted like a flashing blue saber at the intruder.

And then on a certain fall day everything changed. Whether it was when the beeches turned a certain shade of gold, or the maples and oaks wore autumn reds, or whether it was the bite in the wind that gave the signal—no one then or since has ever found out. Perhaps it was just plain squirrel instinct that was responsible. Whatever it was, every squirrel got the same message on the same day, and immediately set out for the South. They paid no more attention to the field of corn than to a tangle of nettles. The forest trembled with their passing. Sandy, who had witnessed many a squirrel migration, told how he had stood on the banks of the Ohio River and watched as squirrels by the thousands swam across.

Schools along the river let out. Boys and men scooped up squirrels by the basketful. Squirrel scalps brought a three-cent bounty in some counties.

"Maybe there won't be any squirrels next year," William hopefully suggested. Perhaps he was thinking of all the time he would have so he could write words.

Jane looked toward the vacated nest in the hollow maple limb. The bluebirds, too, had gone South. "I hope Old Blue and Mrs. Blue come back."

"I'm sure that both the squirrels and bluebirds will return," said Sandy. "It has always been so."

November found a pile of pumpkins beside the McGuffey cabin, unshelled dry beans in the loft (pumpkins and beans had been grown with the corn), the granary filled with unhusked corn, and fodder stacked behind the barn. Now there was more time for lessons. Along with the spelling and writing of words, Anna started William and Jane reading the Bible. William poured over the Book, spelling aloud the words he couldn't figure out. He was fascinated with the idea that words put together on a page could tell a story. He also discovered that once he had figured out a Bible verse so that he could read it, afterward he could say it from memory.

On blizzardy days when Sandy couldn't work in the woods, he carried bushels of unhusked corn from the granary and dumped them on the floor in front of the fireplace. The family gathered around to shuck and shell it, a harsh raspy task for small hands. But the children seemed not to mind the work if Pa told them Indian stories. A story they always asked for, though they'd heard it many times, was the one about his tricking the Indians with an empty gun.

Cornhusks were yanked with doubled energy as Sandy pictured the Indians' surprise attack on General St. Clair's troops in the Maumee country, the savage war whoops, the flailing tomahawks, the scalping knives, and the troops fleeing for their lives. Anna wished Sandy wouldn't make the story so—so bloody sounding, but she guessed it could be no other way when 600 men lost their lives in just minutes. The children imagined themselves fleeing with Sandy up a hill—gun empty and three brightly painted warriors in hot pursuit—only to find the way blocked by a tangle of brush. With him the children whirled to face their pursuers; with him they pointed empty guns (corn cobs made handy substitutes). Hardly had the Indians dived for cover when the cornhuskers clamored, "Tell what happened afterward, Pa." They liked the story's sequel best of all.

"Mind, you work if I tell it."

"Yes, yes, please, Pa."

So Sandy told how one day several years later when he was in the town of Wheeling, West Virginia, a tall long-striding Indian brave stopped him on the street. "'Member me?" he asked.

Sandy had studied the man's face. "No, don't believe I do. Should I?"

The Indian then informed him that he was one of the braves who had chased him up the hill, and added, "You no have gun, we catch."

"We catch?" Sandy repeated. "Are you sure?"

He then challenged the Indian to a race. Down the main street of Wheeling they had raced while onlookers cheered or stared.

"Who won, Pa?" William asked, knowing the answer but wanting to hear it again.

Sandy poured the shelled corn into a deerskin bag. "I won—I won the race and a greater respect for Red men. The Indian grinned and pumped my hand up and down, and said, 'Guess we no catch. You fast runner.'"

January covered the ground with snow, reminding the family that the time had come to burn the trees Pa had girded, that were now dead. The snow on the ground prevented the humus in the soil from burning. Here and there Sandy cut down a tree, piled brush around others to make the fire run, then started the blaze. Tall tongues of flame leaped up into the sky, crackling and roaring.

William, Jane, and Henry brought out their store of buckeyes that they had hoarded for the "big fire." Thrown into the flames the nuts exploded like pistol shot.

Anna made the day special with a picnic supper. The children rolled onions into clay-coated balls which she put to roast along with ash cake—cornbread baked in a covered kettle in hot ashes in the coals at the fire's edge. A feast they would have—juicy onions and hot cornbread dripping with wild honey.

But the fun came to a sudden stop when Jane screamed, "Look! Look! Old Blue's nest is burning!" and burst into tears.

In vain Anna tried to comfort her daughter. "Blue will find another nest. The forest has many trees with hollow branches."

It was William who came up with the suggestion that finally dried Jane's tears. "We'll build Blue a house and nail it to the barn. He'd like it there because the squirrels wouldn't bother him."

After the big fire, a house for Blue and his mate held first interest. What kind of a house should it be? Everyone agreed that the bluebirds would most likely prefer a house such as they had always nested in. So began the search for a hollow branch in which a woodpecker had drilled a hole for an entrance. With Sandy's help, the right branch was found at last, cut from the parent tree, and fastened to the ridgepole of the barn. And not a day too soon!

March brought a deceptive spring and with it Old Blue. When the family discovered his arrival, he had already adopted the new home, subject of course to the approval of his mate when she should come. He sat on a high limb of an elm that overhung the barn and warbled his *Cheer-ie, Cheer-ie*.

And then winter returned to Gravel Hill. For almost a week

the sky poured out a cold sleety intermittent rain. During a let-up Henry, mittened and mufflered, was allowed out for a run down the road and back. And there in the road, half in and half out of an icy puddle, he found Blue. Grabbing up the bird, he raced to the cabin, shouting, "Open the door! Open the door! Blue's drownded."

But Blue was not "drownded." The warmth of the cabin soon revived him. Placed in a slatted box, he was tended with care— Henry stoutly defending his right as keeper—until the weather cleared. On a sunny April day the reluctant keeper lugged the box to the cabin stoop and set Blue free. "'Tisn' t right," he told the watching William, Jane, and little Anna, "to keep a wild bird caged up. Pa says so."

As Blue winged his way to the ridgepole of the barn, he couldn't know he was winging his way into fame, but he was. One day, one of the children who watched him would write a story about him and thousands of children would read it. Had Blue known, fame wouldn't have made a whit of difference in his way of life. He would have gone South every fall just the same, and every spring returned to the nest on the ridgepole of the barn at Gravel Hill— always a little too early.

Perhaps it was because of the recent bird experience that Anna decided on a reading lesson about "not one sparrow falls to the ground," found in the tenth chapter of Matthew. She asked William to read first.

"Couldn't I just say the verses, Ma?"

"You mean you know them by heart?"

"It's easy, Ma. You just read a verse and know it. I know lots of verses."

The light of a long ago wish came into Anna's eyes. "William, I think you are going to be a minister."

Both mother and son instinctively glanced at Sandy for approval. But Sandy was asleep in his chair in the corner beside the fireplace.

CHAPTER THREE

A Buckeye Boy Grows Up

The year 1812. A year for U.S. history books. A year when the United States declared war on Great Britain for "high-handed" searching of American ships and impressment of sailors, and a year of aggressive expansion by Native Americans and British along the Canadian border. But in February 1812, no hint of national conflict had penetrated the forest surrounding the McGuffey's homestead. Their only thought of expansion concerned the one-room cabin in which they had lived for nine years. "We're about to push the logs out of the walls," complained Anna to Sandy.

The family had grown both in size and in number. Three small girls had joined the circle since little Anna—Kathryn, Elizabeth, and a wee lassie with hair as red as Henry's, bringing the count of children to seven. But space wasn't the only commodity Anna had run short of. When the last baby arrived, she'd run out of family girls' names. "Bring the Bible," she told Sandy. "Let it open where it will, and the first woman's name you come to, we give it to the baby."

So Sandy brought the Bible. Its pages lumped together as they turned and finally lay open at Genesis 41. He ran his finger down the page, stopping at verse 45, and read: "Pharaoh . . .

gave him [Joseph] to wife, Asenath."

Anna held the baby close. "Asenath shall be your name, my bonnie bairn, and if folk say they never before heard it, 'tis because they haven't read the Bible through, word for word."

And now Asenath was 7 months old. Soon her little feet would be added to the cabin's already crowded traffic. "A person can't turn around in here without bumping into someone," Anna said, and it was the truth. So it was decided a new room should be built onto the front of the cabin, running its full length. A trap door in the floor of the room would open into the cellar, and the new room would boast a loft with both inside and outside entrances.

William watched Sandy drive pegs into the ground marking out the new room. "May I help with the log-cutting, Pa?"

Sandy hesitated, peg in hand. "You want to tackle the woods? Well, you're a big 11—"

"I'll be 12 in September," William prompted.

"So you will. So you will. I think maybe you are ready to larn the sling o' the ax."

No promotion speech, scholastic and long, ever made an applicant more pleased than Sandy's homely assent which promoted William from guard-of-corn to woodsman's apprentice. To get the feel of his ax, a woodsman, Sandy said, should shape his own ax helve. William worked hard carving his from a length of hickory. The helve must have the proper curve, it must be polished to marble smoothness, and it must fit the ax-head without play.

On a March day, when snow still lay on the ground in dirty patches, William shouldered his ax and followed Sandy into the woods to cut and notch logs for the new room. He soon discovered that Pa was as particular a teacher as Ma. Stance, slant of blade, subtle twist at the end of a stroke to lift the chip clean figured in every swing of the ax—no sloppy work, no dawdling did either parent allow. He felt he had finally achieved when one evening at supper Pa told Ma, "Our firstborn is on his way to a topnotch woodsman." Ma smiled but made no reply.

Only one fault did Pa find with William's work—the irregular rhythm of his swing. "Sometimes you swing with the speed of an experienced old woodpecker, at other times as slow as a fledgling just out of the nest."

William knew the reason but he couldn't tell Pa, for it had to do with reading and Pa, well he didn't take to reading—much. As William chopped he recited to himself whatever he had last read, and the reading set the pace of his ax. Paul's speech to the Athenians on Mars Hill which began, "Ye men of Athens," or Elijah's challenge to King Ahab on Mount Carmel, "Prove ye this day whom ye will serve," brought a shower of chips, but when the discouraged prophet lay under a juniper sighing for death, then the chips slowed to a sprinkle. If being a woodsman barred reading and it might, for Pa came in at night so tired that he slumped into his chair beside the fireplace and almost immediately his chin sank to his chest, William wasn't sure he wanted to be one. Better than anything else, William liked to read.

But to work beside Pa made him feel good. Hadn't Pa been the fastest runner in the army, and wasn't he the strongest man in the neighborhood? Why he had seen Pa grab a bully, a giant of a man, and shake him as Curly would shake a rat. To work beside a man like that made a boy feel that, at last, he was beginning to grow up.

The logs were cut and snaked to the cabin in time for corn planting. After corn planting, the McGuffey manpower, Henry included, concentrated on excavating the cellar for the new room. Sandy hewed a puncheon to bridge the cavernous pit from cabin to yard.

Then on a sultry August day, before even the first log of the new room had been rolled into place, news swept down from the north that put such things as new rooms completely out of mind. The news plunged settlers into a furor of double-barring doors, oiling guns, molding bullets, and posting sentinels. For British troops allied with the powerful Shawnee chief, Tecumseh, and 600 warriors had taken Port Mackinac on Lake Huron and were advancing rapidly south. Would the garrisons at Detroit and Fort Dearborn be able to check the invaders?

A few days later Detroit had surrendered and Fort Dearborn was evacuated. Now the way south lay wide open. Nor did the threat confine itself to the invading forces. How would local Indians react to the reported victories? Was the answer found in the usually friendly Potowatomies' savage ambush of the fleeing Dearborn evacuees, when 12 children in one wagon had been scalped, or in the burning of a cabin on Little Beaver, the entire family tomahawked?

Settlers feared Tecumseh and his warriors far more than they did the British troops. Tecumseh knew every foot of the land, every stream and every path, and he had a personal as well as a tribal grievance to settle. When Tecumseh was 6, his father had been killed in battle by Virginians. When he was 12, Kentuckians had driven the people of his village into the hills to starve. As a young man he had fought in the front rank of warriors that put St. Clair to rout, and he had led the Shawnees against General Wayne, refusing to attend the council fire when defeated chiefs sold Indian hunting grounds.

Instead, Tecumseh had visited tribesmen from the Mississippi to the Maumee to the Great Lakes, assuring them that if they would form an Indian confederacy they could drive White men back across the Alleghenies and regain Indian hunting grounds. He had set up an Indian capitol where Tippecanoe Creek empties into the Wabash. But in Tecumseh's absence, the governor of Indiana, William Henry Harrison, and troops had burned the capitol and scattered the Indians.

"Tecumseh is making a last bid for an Indian kingdom," Sandy told William and Henry as they picketed their horses and cows in a protected area. Tales of stolen stock, rifled granaries, and ransacked cabins were coming in from the Sandusky district. "The wily old chief still assures tribesmen if they will stand together they can yet build an Indian kingdom."

William studied the idea. "Could they, Pa?"

"Too late now. Maybe at one time they could've, but Indian chiefs went their own way, made petty raids, sold land, fought and quarreled with neighboring tribes. Tecumseh has the right idea though. Men have to stand together to build a strong nation."

All day as William swung his ax pushing back the forest by advancing the clearing, Pa's words repeated themselves in his mind: "Men have to stand together to build a strong nation." He would never forget them.

The last thing at night the McGuffeys pulled in the puncheon bridge from across the cellar hole. "Our cabin is the best fortified in the valley," Sandy said. "It has a moat with a drawbridge same as the castles in Scotland."

Pa's like that, William thought. *He's plenty worried but he doesn't let on.*

News of the coming of General William Henry Harrison to take command of American troops against the aggressors burst like a trumpet's reveille after a night of terrifying dreams. Who could better take over than the seasoned old Indian fighter who but a year ago had thwarted Tecumseh at Tippecanoe? He came with a dual commission—to drive British ships off the Lakes and to regain lost territory. Recruits from Ohio, Kentucky, and Indiana marched north on every trail. Every settler—William knew his father's feet itched to join them—stood ready to do voluntary service in what might prove to be a long drawn-out campaign.

But the conflict lasted less than a year. August brought word of victory on Lake Erie. September, a rider galloped into Youngstown with the news that Harrison's troops had joined battle with the British and Indians on the banks of the Canadian Thames. The rider boasted, "Crafty old fox, that Harrison. He launched his attack against red coats 'stead o' red skins. Twenty-two minutes and 'twas all over."

Men threw their hats into the air and cheered. And then someone asked, "What about Tecumseh?"

At mention of the Shawnee chief, the crowd quieted. Yes, what had become of Tecumseh? Though frontiersmen feared him as enemy number one, the fear was mixed with a strange admiration.

"They found him dead," said the rider, "dressed in a British general's uniform and lying in a muck of mud and autumn leaves. I reckon it was seeing their chief cut down that took the fight out o' the Indians."

The rout on the Thames brought the War of 1812 to an end in the Northwest. It had settled not only national problems but ended forever the conflict between ax and arrow in Ohio. The ax unhindered would continue its thud against the forest, making way for farming instead of the hunting the land had known under the arrow.

When Harrison's troops had established themselves between the invaders and settlements south, settlers relaxed in a measure of security. Sandy, during the interim of waiting, thought he'd resume work on the new room, but Anna begged him to finish the road instead. "Jane and William are getting so big. They should have been in a regular school long ago."

And so it came about that with William slinging the ax along with his father the road to Youngstown was completed in time for Reverend Wick's winter term of school. Every day Jane and William walked the 11 miles, five-and-a-half miles each way, to school unless the weather forbade. Then kind Mrs. Wick made room for them at the parsonage on weeknights and they returned home only on weekends.

For William the school day seemed to end before it had barely begun, so thrilled was he to be studying books. When Reverend Wick showed him his library, he could hardly believe there were so many books in the world. And when the pastor said, "You are welcome to read any that you wish," he was so overcome that he barely managed to stammer a thank you. Read any books that he wished? Why, he wished to read them all. He may as well begin with the top shelf and read straight through to the bottom shelf.

William took the books home, one at a time, and read evenings until his candle burned out. Pa devised a candlestick with a plate-size top, that screwed up or down as an organ stool, for him to read by. Ma measured the time he could stay up by length of candle. William looked forward to the hours when he and his book could be alone, shut in by the friendly circle the candle hollowed out of the dark and the silence. Sometimes, when the book was hard to put down, as was *Foxe's Book of Martyrs*, he borrowed a little extra time by throwing a corncob on the coals of the fireplace and crouching on the hearth beside its tiny flame.

William read most books carefully, often memorizing paragraphs and sometimes whole pages. Occasionally he came across a book that he read only sketchily. One such was a thin volume dealing with sundry cures. He wasn't particularly interested in the healing arts. Besides, many of the recommended remedies were already familiar to him. He had helped his mother gather snakeroot and ginseng for fevers, pennyroyal for purifying the blood, and other remedies from nature. Chains of the herbs hung from the cabin rafters, making the loft smell like an apothecary.

But the last chapter of the book produced a title on which he fairly pounced. **"How To Cure A Sleepwalker"** the chapter-head proclaimed in bold type. Here was something to investigate. Henry was a sleepwalker. More than once William had wakened to see his brother standing like a statue on the foot of the bed. Solemnly, slowly, he would step to the floor, and looking neither to the right nor to the left, climb down the ladder to the kitchen. If not prevented, he would open the door, cross the puncheon bridge (it was no longer taken in at night), skirt the barnyard, and then retrace his steps to bed. In the morning he knew nothing of his night's adventure. Fearing that sometime he might come to harm, the family had tried without success to find a cure for Henry's sleepwalking. Did the book have the answer? William read:

"A sleepwalker may be cured of sleepwalking if the one so afflicted suddenly falls into deep water during his perambulation . . ."

William closed the book, laid it aside. The chapter was of no help except that he added the word "perambulation" to his vocabulary; a long word was a find, the longer the better. Henry never perambulated—he supposed that was the verb form of the word—near the lake. William was halfway through *Good's Book of Nature* and had forgotten all about the sleepwalking cure until the day of the electric storm when a cloudburst filled the cellar to overflowing. If only Henry would choose that night to sleepwalk.

But at bedtime Henry didn't appear the least bit perambulatory. He was even too tired to brag much about the bee tree he and Curly had found, and he soon fell asleep. Anyway, William decided to stay awake just in case.

Something wakened William, and he realized that he had slept after all. But a ray of moonlight coming through the loft window revealed Henry, an underwear-clad statue, ready to begin a nightly tour. The big chance had come!

William slipped out of the other side of the bed—thankful that Henry moved slowly—and stole down the ladder. Tiptoeing to the kitchen door, he opened it and closed it behind him. Luck was with him. He had wakened no one. He could only hope

Henry would do as well. Across the puncheon bridge Curly joined him and watched with interest as he eased the far end of the puncheon into the water then drew it to his side of the cellar away from the cabin door. Feat accomplished, he squatted down with an arm around Curly and waited.

The door slowly opened. A moment or two later Henry stepped out into nothingness and plunged deadweight into the water. Curly dived in after him. The barking, yelling, splashing, and laughing (on William's part only) brought the whole family to the scene.

Henry never again walked in his sleep. "But," said William when retelling the episode, "he surely made it hot for me. Ungrateful patient."

From the day that William began attending Reverend Wick's school, Anna turned over the teaching at home to her son. He taught spelling as had she from the now dog-eared *Blue-backed Speller*, which began with one-syllable sounds, ba, be, bi, bo, bu, and carried young learners through ever-lengthening words until they could spell seven-syllable ones such as valetudinarian. The book conveniently explained, "A valetudinarian is a sickly person."

Teaching reading, William had the advantage of Reverend Wick's library. He made a reading folder in which he kept copies of stories and poems for his homeschool reading classes. Favorite poems such as "Twinkle Twinkle Little Star" and "The Lark Is Up" found their way into the folder. His sisters' delight was reward enough for the extra work. They were especially pleased when Ma, having learned the lark poem, wakened them mornings with:

The lark is up to meet the sun,
The bee is on the wing;
The ant its labor has begun,
The woods with music ring.

Shall birds, and bees, and ants be wise,
While I my moments waste?
O let me with the morning rise,
And to my duty haste.

The overburdened Reverend Wick often asked William to teach classes in the parsonage school. The young ones, he observed, never sucked their fingers during William's lessons, and older pupils lingered after class when the gangly boy from Gravel Hill taught them. "You should look to the teaching profession," the pastor advised. William's future was becoming confused. Ma wanted him to be a minister, Pa wanted him to be a woodsman, and now Reverend Wick suggested teaching.

William might be confused as to future profession, but his body had no confusion as to its future size. It patterned him after Pa. Already broad shoulders sat a slim erect frame, and his muscles bulged from swinging the ax. No matter how long Anna made pant legs and coat sleeves, they soon parted company with big feet and big hands.

When the new room was completed, William and Henry moved into the new section of the loft. The outside stair enabled them to be up and out early for morning chores without disturbing the family. Two rooms, a double loft, and a cellar seemed a mansion to their mother, and that summer fulfilled yet another of her dreams. On Sundays the whole family, dressed in their best, rode in the new wagon to Reverend Wick's for church.

Grapes and paw paws were ripening in the forest. William's thoughts turned toward the fall term of school, but he knew that for him attendance would be late if at all. Rails must be split, and a fence built around the extended clearing. And then, two weeks before school began, the way unexpectedly opened. A passer-by, likely a man returning from Harrison's army, stopped at Gravel Hill and offered to work a spell for his keep. Sandy gave him the rail-splitting job. Anna, as pleased as William at the turn of events, made up a bed in the loft for her new roomer-boarder.

But not many days passed before the McGuffeys realized the rail-splitter had an objectionable habit, two in fact. He came in very late at night smelling of corn whiskey. Both Sandy and Anna had been brought up on a strict taste-not, handle-not where liquor was concerned. Anna fretted about the man's influence on the boys. "Can't you say something, Sandy, to show him the evil of his ways. But don't let him go just yet though, William has his heart so set on school."

Before Sandy had figured out an approach, William, tiring of being awakened in the middle of the night, and especially of the obnoxious smell, decided on a reform of his own. No doubt Henry was a partner but the idea was William's. After evening chores he smuggled a rattrap up the outside stair to the loft where he set its steel jaws. Then he placed the trap in the hired man's bed, pulling the quilts taut to hide any tell-tale lump.

He and Henry went to bed but not to sleep. Tense with excitement they lay awake listening to the night sounds that filtered into the loft—the seesawing of frogs, the fiddling of cicadas, the occasional call of a coyote. Finally a heavy step sounded on the stair. Hand squeezed hand under the covers to let the other know its owner had heard. The man climbed uncertainly. A spot of moonlight and the familiar foul smell entered the loft with him. The new cornhusk tick rustled crisply as he sank down on the bed. A boot thumped the floor . . . another boot . . . the grunting sounds of undressing, then a long silence.

Had the man discovered the trap? William ventured a look. No, unsteady fingers were laboring with the buttons of a long white nightshirt. Now—he was getting into bed. William held his breath. He clutched Henry.

THWACK! Straight up and out of bed the man catapulted.

With a yell that shook the rafters, he made the outside entrance in a leap, the bed sheet trailing after. The trap had coupled sheet and nightshirt tail together. Down the stairs, around and around the cabin he raced, shouting something about demons being after him. When Curly joined the chase, the man ran as if the whole underworld were in pursuit.

Before daylight the rail-splitter left Gravel Hill, swearing that he wouldn't stay another night under the same roof with that Bill McGuffey.

William was sharpening his ax on the grindstone when Sandy spoke his name. "William."

"Yes, Pa."

"Since last night"—Sandy put his hand to his mouth and coughed. "Since last night," he repeated, "you know what's expected of you."

"Yes, Pa, a rail fence. I'm grinding my ax."

He watched his father walk away. Pa hadn't been too angry with him after all. The corners of his mouth had twisted into what might have been a grin had he not coughed. And now as he strode toward the barn, a muttering floated back that sounded like, "A good riddance, a good riddance."

William attacked the ash logs with a vengeance. If he worked very hard, perhaps he could make the last half of the school term. To split a log he made slits along its length with his ax. Next he inserted hardwood wedges in the slits, then pounded them in deeply with a maul. The log responded with a straight clean break. In the same way he slit each half of the log, and so on. He figured he could average 75 rails a day.

Reverend Wick sent books home with Jane, as well as word to William as to where he might borrow other books. After working all day William often walked miles to borrow a book. As special compensation the pastor promised to start him in Latin when he returned to school. William was jubilant.

Sandy saw no sense in such folderol. Wasn't English good enough?

But Anna insisted that Latin was the mark of an educated man. "'Tis the root of our language, I've heard tell." But Sandy who'd had to grub far too many roots out of the ground, could not appreciate roots of any kind. They cluttered up a man's living, he figured, whether of the mental or the material sort.

As winter turned into spring, and spring into summer, a tenseness settled over the McGuffey household revealed in worry wrinkles between Anna's eyes and an increasing silence on Sandy's part. The final land payment was due, but they had no cash to pay it and no prospect of making any. Since the war, settlers had moved west by the thousands. Peltry was no longer available as in the early days, and significant out-of-state markets did not yet exist. Anna's butter brought three cents a pound in Youngstown, and eggs, only four cents a dozen. Everyone grew what everyone else did. A family could live off the land but the land must be paid for in cash.

When a stranger, a businesslike-looking man, rode up to the McGuffey cabin about noon one day in late July, Anna met him at the door with obvious nervousness. She no doubt feared he might be a land agent come to collect or to foreclose. The man introduced himself as a resident of West Union (Calcutta) and had stopped by to discuss a certain matter.

Courtesy demanded that Anna invite him to stay for dinner, which she did, saying her husband would be coming from the woods shortly. She called Henry to take care of the man's horse, and offered her guest a chair near the door where a bit of breeze entered the steamy hot cabin. Jane added a pewter plate to the wooden trenchers already on the table. The little girls hid in convenient corners.

The gentleman took the proffered chair, mopped his forehead with a red kerchief, and explained his coming. Early that morning he had visited Reverend Wick in the interest of securing a teacher for the West Union school. The reverend had suggested a William McGuffey, William Holmes McGuffey, and directed him to Gravel Hill. Did the young man live here?

Anna assured him that he did, and that he would be coming with his father to dinner, but that he could hardly be called a young man. "Our William," she said, "has taught his brother and sisters, and has helped the pastor in his school, but he is only a lad, not 14 until September."

The man from West Union shook his head and sighed, intimating he'd wasted his morning. Again he mopped his forehead. "Too young," he said. "Fourteen's too young to teach."

Just then Sandy and William came in. The stranger arose and introduced himself as a passerby, making no mention of the teaching business.

"West Union, you say? Well, well, you've got a piece yet to go. Set up and eat," invited Sandy.

William, from the moment of entering the cabin, felt himself being scrutinized by the stranger. Though crops, weather, and the recent war were discussed by his father and the guest, every time he looked up from his plate he saw the man's eyes on him. In fact, they fairly bored into him. He quickly finished his food and asked to be excused.

"Hold on, young fellow," said the man from West Union. "I have something to talk over with you, a proposition to make." And then he repeated all that he had told Anna, adding, "I understand you are but 14."

"Going on 14, sir."

Again the eyes sized William up and down. "You look all of 17, and with that build"—his eyes twinkled—"you know the saying about teaching, 'No lickin' no larnin'."

And before the man rode away from Gravel Hill, William, with his parents' consent, had signed his name to a contract drawn up between the teacher and 23 families of West Union. The contract read:

"Master McGuffey agrees to hold a four month session of school on Lot 4 West Union and to tutor all pupils at two dollars each per term commencing the first Monday of September, 1814, Anno Domino."

When the school representative of West Union shook hands good-bye, addressing him as "Teacher McGuffey," William felt almost grown up. He felt even more so when after the man left, Ma wept. He couldn't imagine why. Never had he felt less like weeping. He did some quick mental arithmetic. The signers had promised 48 pupils. Forty-eight times two dollars was $96. Of course something would be taken out for board, but even at that . . . He pictured the day he would bring the money home and hand it to Pa toward the land payment.

That was the day he would be grown up, a responsible man of the family.

CHAPTER FOUR

Roving Teacher . . . Trustees' Exams

A gain the month was August, but in name only, for the year
was 1816, "the year without a summer," also called the year
"everybody froze." June, July, and August brought frost and sometimes ice to the fields of Ohio. Crops died before they had half
grown. Even the squirrels paid little attention to the ruined corn.
Food would be rationed in many a cabin the following winter.

William and Henry were plowing a new clearing. Henry drove
the team. William wrestled the plow which bucked like a mustang
when it struck a giant oak root, and balked like a mule when its
point became enmeshed in an underground warp and woof of elm,
beech, and hackberry. Breakfast seemed hours ago, because it was.
Both boys felt hollow clean through, but they didn't go to the
cabin for lunch. A midwife was there attending to a birthing.

Jane was a wonderfully welcome sight when, at last, she approached the clearing carrying a jug in one hand and a basket
in the other. While the boys gulped cider and wolfed cornbread and cold meat, she told them that they had a new little
brother. He was a healthy baby, too, judging by his squall. Ma
had named him after Pa. And already Pa had written his name
in the family Bible—"Alexander Hamilton McGuffey, born
August the 13th, 1816."

Before unhitching that evening, William had made up his mind that there was one mouth too many in the McGuffey family for Pa to feed, especially a big one like his. As soon as Henry and he finished the plowing, he would strike out on his own and try his luck as a roving teacher. The regret at leaving home was partly offset by a feeling of independence, but more so by the challenge of earning tuition money to further his education. He had his sights set on Old Stone Academy at Greersburg (Darlington) Pennsylvania, 30 miles from Gravel Hill.

Early on a frosty morning, with a shawl about his shoulders and a pack containing clothes, reading folder, and Bible (an early sixteenth birthday gift from Ma) strapped to his back, he bade farewell to the family and started on his adventure toward higher education. His mother's "God bless you" followed him down the McGuffey Road, the road his ax had helped build.

He had no teacher's certificate. None was needed in the early 1800s. A country school usually began with parents deciding something should be done about the ignorance of their children. One family would give a plot of land, others cut logs, and together they raised up a log cabin with fireplace and chimney. They furnished it with greased-paper windows, seats of split logs, and a table on a raised platform for the teacher. Under the windows other split logs, flat side up, were fastened to the walls for writing desks. The better schools boasted puncheon floors, while others had only packed earth. Cabin completed, a roving teacher was hired, or someone in the community who could spell tolerably well, write a fair hand, and maybe do a bit of ciphering. Books were a hit and miss variety and, outside the Bible, so few that in those years Ohio was designated "bookless."

William soon discovered that circumstances had vastly changed since the day he signed the contract with West Union. Cash, scarce even then, had become almost nonexistent. The only chance some schools had of operating depended on hiring a local farmer as teacher who could haul away tuition fees in his wagon the last day of school or on whose homestead the tuition could be worked out. In schools that paid cash the tuition might be as low as 50 cents for a three-months' terms. At that, it was expected a goodly part of the teacher's salary would be cared for by his "boarding around."

To board around meant the teacher must move from one pupil's home to another, staying a prescribed length of time at each. That one cabin was close by the school and another far away seemed not to influence the arrangement, nor did creek fordings, hills, swamps, or the quantity or quality of food a family might be able to provide. In one home he might be feasted on cornbread and venison, while in another a tough old turkey gobbler, roasted the day of his coming, might outlast his stay.

Sleeping arrangements demanded adjustment also. The more well-to-do cabins had lofts where the teacher slept on a corn-husk mattress with the boys of the family and sometimes had the luxury of a lumpy feather tick for covering. Then the nights were fairly comfortable though the boys squirmed and kicked, and snow sifted in under the eaves. One-room cabins with no loft presented a different situation. At bedtime, when teacher stayed with the family, he and the older male members stepped out-of-doors, rain or snow making no difference, while the women undressed. The blowing out of the candle was the signal for those outside to enter, undress in the dark—the fire had been banked—and roll up in a blanket on the floor.

Country school boards were impressed with William's qualifications: that he had attended Reverend Wick's school, that he had studied Latin, could cipher to the rule of three (ratio and proportion) though they probably had no idea what it meant, and that he had had teaching experience. These facts qualified him scholastically, and his build qualified him physically, for the prevailing idea of education was that of the West Union representative, "No lickin' no larnin'!" As a farmer tamped in the seed when planting hills of corn and pumpkins, so a teacher must tamp in the learning, else it wouldn't "ketch."

When William's pupils reported few whippings, parents questioned if the school board had hired a lackadaisical teacher. But that could hardly be, else the rowdies would be cutting capers. Time would tell. Anyway, they were safe tuition-wise, for teachers were never paid until the last day of school in case they might take a notion to leave.

Truth was that William, in character with his Scotch Presbyterian ancestry, held to a code of discipline as rigid as a ramrod. He tolerated no "levity." He told his pupils, ages ranging from 5 to 25, that so much to learn and so little time in which to learn it, left no time for foolishness. How did the pupils react? A significant statement follows William's teaching trail, "The pupils came early to school and lingered after."

He possessed an ability that won him favor as well as good discipline, the ability to coach in the favorite sports of the day—declamation—"or oratin'" pupils termed it if teacher were not around to insist on the i-n-g—and spelldowns. The pieces which William had memorized and practiced as he swung his ax now came in handy. Before and after school he helped aspiring William Tells to "articulate with proper voice and gesture," and youthful Patrick Henrys to thunder, "Give me liberty or give me death!" He helped the Svensons and Schultzes with their problem of learning English, and he supervised spelling workouts.

William's heart went out to the younger children who sat the long day through, swinging feet from the too-high backless benches. As for tools for learning, they had the least of all—perhaps a badly-chewed speller passed down to them by older brothers and sisters and the occasional *New England Primer*, a gloomy little catechism of the Puritan faith. Some of the youngsters had already sat through two terms of school, spelling the same words again and again—with no reading lessons at all.

Oh, for a set of readers, readers with stories about dogs and horses, work and play, Bible stories too. Surely someday someone would publish a set of such readers. William improvised as best he could with homemade charts, and supplemented the scanty fare with stories and poems copied from his reading folder.

Older pupils read from the Bible and the few reading lessons found in the spelling books. They took turns writing at the wall desks, laboriously imitating the copy William set. In arithmetic each progressed as he was able. Spelling was studied with zest in lieu of spelldowns. History and geography were oral and depended on the teacher's knowledge. Here again Reverend Wick's library and William's ability to memorize paid dividends.

A three-month term crammed full of activity went quickly by. With earnings so meager that after the boarding around he could tie the few coins in the corner of a kerchief, William went on his way seeking another school. Perhaps to the west times were better. When he came across an empty school building, he canvassed the neighborhood to find out if families desired a term of school, and if there were enough paying pupils to make it worthwhile. If so he stayed. If not he trudged on.

After two years of intermittent searching and teaching, with the searching intervals growing ever longer—William gave up. He couldn't make it. Ohio was flooded with scrip but little cash. (The next year, 1819, brought a financial panic.) Anything he earned at one school was used up before he located another. Defeated and discouraged, he set out for Gravel Hill. Old Stone Academy was beyond his attainment.

Up the McGuffey Road . . . and then home. He hid his feelings as he greeted the family who welcomed him enthusiastically. Pa said he couldn't have timed his coming better, for he needed a rail splitter. Standing back to back, he and Henry were the same height. Jane, who had passed her nineteenth birthday, blushed when he asked about a certain neighbor boy. The little girls, ages 7 to 14, hovered near to hear all that he had to tell. Two-year-old Alec simply took possession of the big brother who had come walking up the road, and refused to be separated. He rode on William's shoulder as he toured the farm, considered William's foot his private hobbyhorse, insisted on sitting beside him at the supper table, and wailed a protest when carried off to bed.

At last William and his mother were alone, as the other family members were occupied with evening chores. Anna began the conversation. "Well, my son, how goes it?"

William recounted his whole discouraging experience, discouraging as to funds, for he had enjoyed the teaching. "It's no use reaching for the impossible, Ma. I may as well begin looking for a homestead and start slinging the ax."

"If ye have faith, as a grain of mustard seed," Anna quoted, "nothing shall be impossible unto you." She emphasized each word with both head and hand. "The Almighty can overrule, William."

"Perhaps the Almighty is overruling," William argued. "Maybe I am not supposed to continue my education. Maybe I'm not cut out to be a minister." But Anna did not agree.

William went to bed early, more to be alone than to rest. His mother's words had shaken him. When Henry came up the stairs, he feigned sleep. Later he heard his father come into the cabin. He heard the clunk of mugs on the table in the room below and knew his mother had brewed a nightcap of sassafras tea. He could picture his parents as they sat sipping the scalding liquid, Pa's head nodding between slurps, Ma as alert as if it were morning. Did she never tire? He heard her ask something in a low muffled voice.

A mug clunked firmly, decisively onto the table. His father's answer was neither low nor muffled. "No, there's no money for fancy schoolin'. 'Tis all we can do to send the others to grammar school."

Again his mother spoke, and again his father answered, this time gently, "Lass, ye should have married the schoolmaster back home."

Footsteps . . .

Silence in the room below.

Sleep was blurring William's thinking when once more he became conscious of his mother's voice. This time it came from out-of-doors, from the direction of the silver maple. By its intensity he knew she was laying her problem, or rather his problem, before the Director of Destinies. What a mother. What a faith!

Next morning at breakfast, William and Sandy were discussing homesteads when they were interrupted by a knock on the door. Sandy got up from the table, pulled the latchstring, which was still inside from the night, and opened the door. A clergyman, so indicated by his white cambric cravat, stood on the stoop, his horse tied to the hitching post beyond. He introduced himself as Thomas E. Hughes from Greersburg, Pennsylvania, principal of Old Stone Academy.

William glanced at his mother. She flashed him an "I told you so."

Sandy invited the reverend to "come in and sup." He introduced him to the family who had risen at a signal from their mother. She was last to be introduced since she had stepped to the cupboard to fetch a bowl for their guest's porridge.

"Madam McGuffey," said Reverend Hughes, "I owe you an apology." Color reddened his neck above the swathes of cravat. "I'm not in the habit of eavesdropping on people's conversation with each other, much less on their private conversation with the Lord," he began. "But last night after dusk when riding past this place, I overheard a mother laying before the Almighty a son's problem in obtaining an education." The color in his neck fused upward. "I confess I stopped to listen since education is my business. And I beg your pardon though I can't say that I'm sorry."

Now it was Anna's turn to blush. "I did not mean to—to be forward, praying outdoors, and the like."

"Forward?" questioned Reverend Hughes, and helped himself from the bowl of steaming cornmeal porridge she passed him. "Not at all. More folk would do well to hold their devotions under the stars. No sham or false pride can abide the stars looking on. 'Twas Abraham's favorite temple." He chuckled. "'Tis a good place to obtain promises, too. The patriarch, you will remember, found it so."

As the meal progressed, the guest explained that during the past weeks he had been canvassing the countryside for worthy students. Returning to Youngstown last evening, since the hour was late, he would no doubt have ridden past Gravel Hill without realizing an eligible student resided on its slope, had not a voice out of the dusk informed him so. He turned to William. "This morning I retraced the five miles to invite you to enroll in Old Stone Academy."

"But sir, I have no funds for—"

The reverend held up his hand. "Remember, I know the whole story down to the smallest detail. Your mother told it well."

A fortnight later, when Reverend Hughes rode toward the Pennsylvania border, William rode along beside him, his few belongings in a saddlebag. Arrangements had been made for him to do janitor work in the Greersburg church for his tuition and chores at the Hughes' home for his board and room. Sandy did not object to William's going. Hadn't William taken to the woods when his father wanted him, when the boy would've rather been studying books? A turnabout, he figured, was fair enough. Besides, the school let out in April so that students could help with their folks' farm work. He lent William the horse that he might come home now and then. The only McGuffey who objected to William's going was small Alec, who howled lustily to be taken along.

On first approach Old Stone Academy, a two-story structure built of roughhewn stone, appeared austere. Its bare four-pane windows coldly searched all corners, but the door opened in. And when one entered, the 20-inch-thick walls that had been forbidding from without gave a sense of granite security from within. The windows looked out on a village of weathered log cabins, the smoke of their chimneys speaking of warmth and hospitality.

Here, for two years William attended classes. Here, Principal Hughes "Latined him" for college until he could think in Latin. Hughes "crammed him" for teachers' examinations so he might teach in town schools which paid higher wages than country schools, and earn his way through college. William studied as only a teacher turned pupil can study. He memorized whole books of the Bible, pages of history and of the classics. He practiced elocution in the woods. When an old raccoon came evening after evening, sitting meditatively in the crotch of a maple listening to him declaim "Anthony's Speech at the Death of Caesar," William figured himself ready to reach the dullest minds.

As agreed, William worked out the three-dollar-a-term tuition sweeping, dusting, scrubbing the church where Reverend Hughes preached on Sundays. He carried wood, water, and coal for Mrs. Hughes, milked the cow, and tended the stable for the privilege of eating the students' bill of fare—coffee and bread with butter for breakfast, bread with meat or potatoes for the midday meal, mush and milk for supper. The cost to students was 75 cents a week.

When William completed his course at Old Stone Academy, he felt himself quite educated, at least equal to facing the examining boards of town schools. Confidently, he applied for the position of headmaster in the new brick school of Warren, county seat of Trumbull County, and 14 miles up the Mahoning River from Youngstown. The trustees accepted his application and set the date of examination.

Leaving Youngstown, William rode northwest on the old Indian trail that followed the winding Mahoning. The day was lazily warm. A distance upriver the pungent smell of sulphur reminded him that he was near the salt spring where he and Sandy had boiled down many a bushel of salt. He turned aside to have a look. Three Indians, two squaws and a brave, were tending a smudgy fire under a salt kettle. The fire tenders bore no resemblance to the braves of Sandy's Indian stories, nor to the proud Tecumseh. One of the squaws held out a scrawny hand for a copper. White men's firewater had reduced them to miserable beggars. He must remember to add this scene when he cautioned pupils on "Taste not, touch not, handle not."

The thought of pupils brought him back to his present mission. As he rode on he speculated on the trustees' examination. On what subjects would they quiz him? If on Bible, Latin, or the classics, he knew he couldn't fail.

He pulled up in front of the new brick building. Warren had a right to be proud of its educational center. He dismounted, tied his horse to a hitching post, wiped the dust from his shoes, adjusted his cravat, and entered the building. He was early, but the trustees had already assembled and were gathered around a long oak table. The trustee with whom he had corresponded introduced him to the other members, giving a brief account of each—the part of the country from which he came, school attended, and present business.

Pangs of uncertainty nagged William when he learned that two of the trustees were Yale graduates. Their broadcloth suits in contrast to his homespun made him feel his backwoods origin. By token of the same contrast would they ask questions on a university level or on the curriculum level he would be teaching? As he studied their faces, he knew the answer.

William had never wanted to get away from anywhere as he did from the Warren school that day. He could barely refrain from bolting as the Yale men questioned him on subjects he had never studied, some he had never heard of. But he kept his chair, respectfully answering as best he could. When the interview was over he made himself shake hands, walk calmly to the door, and close it slowly behind him.

He knew he had failed, miserably failed. No one need tell him. But strangely he felt more stimulated than depressed. The Yale men with their questions had unwittingly given him glimpses into new fields of learning, like doors along a corridor that opened for a moment and then closed. He would go to college. How, he didn't know, but he would go.

CHAPTER FIVE

"Look Well to Your Seed, Look Well to Your Soil"

To most Ohioans, Warren meant "a very pleasant town" on the Mahoning River, but to William it meant the turning point of his life though it was very unpleasant at the time. Had he not failed the trustees' examination he might have settled down as headmaster of a town school—the position was attractive—instead of hurdling the obstacles of a college education. Now, nothing short of college would do.

Again he took to the road as a roving teacher. This time, bolstered by an academy background, he applied for town schools, most of which were still of the log cabin variety. He was right in the assumption that few boards would give examinations on a Yale graduate level. One of his first town schools was in a village north of East Liverpool, almost in the shadow of Old Stone Academy.

The fall he turned 20, William had earned sufficient funds to enroll in Washington College, Washington County, Pennsylvania. Arrangements were made for him to live in the home of the president, Reverend Andrew D. Wylie, honor graduate of Jefferson College and 10 years William's senior. The two of them would walk together the six miles to the college each morning. William signed up for five courses: Latin, Greek, Hebrew, ancient history, and the all-important mental philosophy, questions on which he had been forced to answer with silence at the Warren examination. And he determined that the biblical slogan, "Out of weakness were made strong," would be his experience.

"Quite a furrow you're attempting to plow," commented Wylie.

William grinned. "I've plowed forest clearings, sir." Then, realizing that the comparison meant nothing to his friend who, reared in an English village, had had no experience with giant oak and elm roots, he added, "It is a load, but I'm strong."

Stretch his money as he would, William could not make it cover all of the necessary textbooks. Those he could not purchase he would attempt to memorize or copy on limited loan. History he could memorize, but the Greek grammar he would need for reference. So he sharpened a quantity of goose quills to the finest of points, and each night after the next day's lessons were learned, he worked on the Greek grammar, copying the text complete with explanations, declensions, conjugations, and rules. His pen marched across the page in horizontal lines that curved neither up nor down; it formed columns as perpendicular as a plumb line. Often he worked on past midnight.

Early one morning a tap sounded on his door. Andrew Wylie, dressed in the classic white nightshirt of the day and sheltering the flickering flame of a candle with his hand, opened the door in answer to William's, "Come."

"I know it's none of my business, McGuffey. You are burning your own candle, your own wood, your own energy, but aren't you ever going to bed? It's almost 3:00 o'clock, and we leave for school at 5:00."

"I'll turn in now," William acquiesced, "but don't worry about my overworking. I can take it. I've no choice but to double up on time. I'm entering college at an age I should be graduating."

"A diploma in a sickly hand doesn't count for much," Wylie dryly observed and closed the door.

William laid down his quill and stood up. His legs were stiff from long sitting, and a spot between his shoulders burned. *I'll suffer no harm*, he assured himself. *I'm tough like Pa, and like him, after a few nods I'll snap back into fine fettle.*

William finished the year with honors. And after replenishing his funds with a term of teaching, he enrolled for another year of college as taxing and as grueling as his first. But before the semester ended he learned the hard truth that some gains are loss. His body rebelled against the continual punishment. A fever he could not shake grew progressively worse. His thinking dulled; his phenomenal memory hardly retained a new conjugation overnight. Instead of the "sick hand" that Wylie had cautioned against, William feared a sick head was to be his lot.

"A complete rest," Professor Wylie now prescribed, and advised his going home for a few weeks or months. This time William followed his counsel.

At home, Anna put him to bed and dosed him with all the remedies she knew, but the fever ran its course. Finally there came a day when his mind emerged from its blur and began to focus again. Color seeped back into his face, his skin became moist. William would never forget the first time after his illness that he attempted to run his hand, in characteristic gesture, through his thick hair. His hand slid over a pate as bald as an old man's.

Anna laughed at his startled look. "'Tis the way with fevers. Your hair will grow again."

Five-year-old Alec, petulant at being barred from the sick bed, was now permitted access. Soon big brother and little brother were roaming the out-of-doors together. They watched the bluebirds, no doubt offspring of Old Blue, feeding their young in the hollow-limb nest atop the barn; they made toy boats and sailed them on the lake; they joined Anna, who knitted on sunny days under the silver maple, for story sessions.

William, whose hand was accustomed to copying classical Greek, could, if slate and slate pencil were urged upon him, produce hilarious small-boy laughter with his drawings.

"There I have drawn a pig and a hen and a duck.

"Why, the pig has two legs and the duck has four.

"Well, I can rub out two of the duck's legs and give them to the pig.

"There now I will draw a man with a whip in his hand. The man has come to put the pig in the pen.

"Why the man is not as tall as the pig. I must rub them all out for they are not well done."

Anna laid down her knitting and watched the two heads bent over the slate, the one still bald from fever, the other a mop of brown curls. Her eldest and her youngest were having a merry time. "William," she interrupted before he got to the moral of the story, not that she didn't believe in moral lessons—she most emphatically did—but because an idea had occurred to her.

"Yes, Ma." The bald head turned her way.

"You have a way with young ones. Why don't you teach Alec his letters?"

And so Alec's start toward a college education began under the silver maple with "A is for ax, B is for box."

Not all of William's time was spent with Alec though the youngster would have had it that way. He brought his muscle into tone by helping Pa and Henry and brother-in-law Joseph (Jane had married the "certain" neighbor boy, Joseph Stewart, of her blushing days) with fence building and corn planting. He and Henry exchanged confidences in the loft at bedtime. Henry looked forward to an apprenticeship with a doctor in Pennsylvania. Both felt guilty at leaving Pa with the farm. Both were thankful for a brother-in-law who had a leaning toward agriculture.

When William attempted to catch up on his studies, he found he would have to get spectacles, so an order was sent to an eastern mail-order house. The evening the spectacles arrived the whole family watched the unpacking and the trying on. The small rectangular lens, fitted with steel rims and steel bows, sat quite far down on his nose, magnifying the print of a book when he looked down, but enabling him to look over them at the interested family. The fever had left him permanently bald on the front part of his head, making his already high forehead appear still higher. Sandy said the spectacles made him look like "Judge Hitchcock, the circuit court rider." Henry came up with "Professor," but Anna insisted on "Reverend."

Dawn hadn't yet begun to light the October sky when William closed the loft door behind him. Carrying his boots, he felt his way down the outer loft stair hoping he hadn't wakened the family, especially Alec who always begged to go with him. Farewells had been said the evening before. Once more he was setting out to resume the plan of alternately teaching subscription schools and attending college.

He wasn't surprised when his mother joined him at the stable. He would have been surprised had she not. She brought more corn cake and another small cheese to add to his lunch. While he grained and saddled his horse, she talked enthusiastically of college and the ministry. She steadied the saddlebag as he secured it with a length of deer thong to the saddle. Bless her, she never made the going away hard. On the contrary, she gave a light push of confidence. And always her "God bless you" followed him down the trail.

William rode with a slack rein allowing his horse to warm up gradually. His thoughts naturally turned toward schools. For a year now he had been a man with a vote, but the vote he would most like to cast hadn't yet even spawned an issue. He would like to vote a triple bill that assured every boy and girl in the West a grammar school education, under a trained teacher, in a proper building. Subscription schools—he shook his head—

didn't measure up. Families were so large they couldn't afford to send all of the children at one time. The Adams and Abigails had to alternate with the Seths and Sarahs. William tightened the reins. Youngsters didn't have a chance, not half a chance. He pressed his horse into a gallop. Teachers ought to be trained, grammar schools ought to be free, in fact, compulsory. If ever he had a chance to speak up . . .

Southward William rode through a carnival of October colors. Some 18 or 20 miles along the trail, the sun shining directly from overhead and a hollow feeling in his stomach reminded him he should stop for lunch. A zesty aroma of apples emphasized the fact and brought him to a halt beside an orchard fenced with a crude brush fence. He was not at all surprised to find the orchard although the area consisted of undeveloped land. Trails for the most part followed rivers, and one could hardly ride a half day along any river in Ohio without coming upon such an orchard. The state had more apples than money, and the apples were free.

William hobbled his horse to graze, then climbed the brush fence and filled his pockets with the yellow and red fruit. He climbed back again and spread his lunch out on a log. Cornbread, cheese, and apples—what better combination! When he bowed his head and gave thanks, an extra clause to his customary grace asked to be included: "And thank you, Lord, for Johnny Appleseed."

Johnny Appleseed (Jonathan Chapman) traveled extensively in Ohio before and during William's roving teacher days. School children had told William many a tale about the scarecrow of a man who planted apple trees and who talked of the road to heaven. They told how in the springtime Johnny Appleseed, wearing a coffee sack for a coat, and tin mush pot for hat, came floating down the Ohio River with two canoes lashed together and filled with apple pulp from the cider mills of Pennsylvania. They told how he paddled up the rivers of Ohio and planted apple seeds in clearings where he thought settlers most likely to come, how he fenced his plantings with brush, and returned each year to tend them, bringing a supply of tracts that told of the way to heaven. Whether Johnny advised men on planting Russets, Pippins, and Live-forevers, or on attaining heaven, his counsel was always the same: "Look well to your seed, look well to your soil."

William took a Barlowe jackknife from a trouser pocket, opened its one blade, and halved the apples. Though Johnny Appleseed ate no meat nor would he kill a living thing, not even a mosquito, the living things didn't hesitate to eat or inhabit his apples. "Better to cut an apple and find a whole worm," so an old saying advised, "than to bite into one and find a half worm." Lunch prepared, William took from a shirt pocket his spectacles and a recent letter from Professor Wylie. What could be more pleasant than sitting beside the trail on a sunny day eating lunch and reading a letter from a friend, especially when the letter ended, "You are missed at Washington College. Hurry back as soon as your health will permit."

William folded the letter and returned it and the spectacles to his shirt pocket. He snapped the Barlowe blade shut and returned the knife to his trouser pocket, then repacked his lunch bag and caught up his horse. It was good to be missed, good to be wanted, but before he could return to Washington College, he would have to have something more in his pockets than spectacles, letter, and jackknife.

Resuming the trail, it was now Johnny Appleseed's counsel to which the horse's hoofs clopped a rhythm, "Look well to your seed, look well to your soil." *Good advice for a teacher*, William mused. *No better soil than a child's mind, no better seed than honesty, honor, industry, and faith.* In his reading folder he had collected story packets of such seed.

In the fall of 1825, before his final semester preceding graduation from Washington College, William contracted to teach the grammar school of Paris, Kentucky. It was at this school, held in a former smokehouse, that an impressive visitor stopped by one late-November afternoon. The visitor was tall and raw-boned, had kindly eyes and spoke with a Scotsman's burr. He did not immediately state the reason of his visit, but introduced himself as Robert Hamilton Bishop, formerly of Edinburgh, but now acting as head of the new Miami University at Oxford, Ohio. Would Teacher McGuffey please continue the afternoon session in his usual manner.

William introduced Reverend Bishop—all university presidents were reverends—to his pupils who arose and bowed in the approved manner. He gave his guest a chair and, as requested, continued with the usual afternoon program. But he couldn't prevent curiosity from creeping into his thinking. *Why had the man come? Did he merely wish to see how schools in America compared with schools in Scotland? Or was there some other motive?* His mind harked back to a couple of other mysterious visitors, the man from West Union who came with a school contract when he was a boy of 14 and Reverend Hughes who came to invite him to Old Stone Academy when he was 18. *Could it be . . .? No.* He put the thought out of his mind.

School closed with the twenty-third Psalm repeated in unison. The pupils filed to the cloakroom for coats and lunch pails, then lined up out-of-doors from the tallest to the least, facing the schoolhouse. William invited Reverend Bishop to accompany him to the door for final dismissal.

The pupils bowed. "Good night, Mister McGuffey. Good night, Reverend Bishop." Teacher and visitor returned the bow and the "Good night." The lines backed away a few paces, then with shouts and whoops that made housewives all over town say, "It must be 4:00 o'clock," they broke rank and boys scuffling, girls arm in arm, they started for home.

Reverend Bishop chuckled. "Whether this side of the Atlantic, or the other, children are the same. I have eight of them myself."

The two men went back into the schoolroom. The reverend commended William on the orderly session, then pointing to the books on his desk said, "Although you teach reading, writing, and ciphering, I notice that Latin, Greek, and Hebrew grammars occupy conspicuous space among your books."

William started to explain but his visitor interrupted, saying he already knew of his attendance at Washington College, his scholarship, his teaching, and speaking ability. "I first heard of you," he said, "while soliciting students for Miami. Patrons mentioned an unusual teacher. They said that their children begged to go to school early and asked to stay after school."

And now Reverend Bishop told the reason for his coming. The head of Ancient Languages at Miami University had accepted a position elsewhere beginning the first of the year, leaving the chair at Miami vacant. Would Mr. McGuffey consider filling the vacancy at a salary of $600.

Unrelated thoughts crowded William's mind, clamoring for attention: *six hundred dollars, a hundred more than Pa paid for the homestead!* But he hadn't completed college. If he left now, would he ever get back and graduate? He had worked toward the ministry, not the teaching of languages. He had promised his mother . . . what would Professor Wylie say?

He asked for time to consider.

Reverend Bishop apologetically said there was no time since the other teacher would be leaving the first of the year. He must have his answer immediately.

William still held out for time. He had to have the counsel of two people—Wylie's and his mother's. The one he could contact by letter, his mother he must talk to face to face. In the end Miami's president conceded a short interim for

William to think over the proposition, shook his hand, mounted his horse, and rode away.

William wrote to Professor Wylie, got a substitute for the Kentucky school, packed his saddlebags, and began the long trek to Youngstown in drizzly, gray weather. At Limestone he took the ferry across the rain-pocked Ohio. On the trail again, rain beat against his face and his horse slewed in the mud. The wind blew as if determined to strip the forest of its last lingering leaf. He rode until late and was finally guided by a dog's barking and his horse's instinct to a cabin where he was made welcome for the night. Frontier folk gladly exchanged lodging for news from the outside. Next day the rain gave way to a pale winter sun.

Days later it was early candlelight when William turned his mount into the McGuffey Road. The horse pricked up his ears, quickened his gait, nickered. William slapped the black shoulder. "Five more miles, old fellow, and we'll be home . . . home!" Not since childhood had he felt so excited. Never had he come home this time of year, and never with such news. His coming would be a total surprise. He wished that Henry were riding along beside him, but Henry had married and settled down to a combination medical and farming career in a town south of the Ohio.

Nearing the homestead, the horse whinnied and was answered. William slipped from the saddle and led him, placing a hand on the animal's nose. "You may want to announce your coming, but I want mine to be a surprise."

When the horse whinnied, William had expected the cabin door to open, but it hadn't. At the barn he stabled and fed his mount midst a blur of welcoming nickers. Then, directed by the light from a window, he approached the cabin. There was no dog to announce his coming. Old Curly had long since lived out his life span and no other dog had taken his place. Pausing on the stoop, William listened to the homey sounds from within—conversation, the rattle of dishes, the coffee mill. The mill's grinding explained why his horse had not been heard.

He pulled the latchstring, opened the door, stepped inside. There was a moment of stunned silence. "William!" Anna gasped, her hand clutching the mill. "Are you—are you sick?"

"Never felt better in my life, Ma." He gave her a kiss and a hug. The family came out of its shock with laughter, more hugs, comments, and questions.

"I thought I must be dreaming," said Little Anna, and introduced her farmer husband, Nehemiah Harris.

William gripped his father's calloused hand. "How goes it, Pa, with your grown-up sons deserting you?"

"'Tis nae too bad so lang as the lassies brang hame the farmer laddies." Sandy found Scottish words more expressive when moved.

William finally got to the tugging on his sleeve. "How long can you stay?" Alec eagerly asked.

"Oh, maybe a week." William looked about the group. In every pair of eyes he read the same question—what had brought him home?

"Suppose we all sit down and I'll tell you why I've come." It pleased William that Alec, though 9 and tall for his age, jostled for a place on the floor nearest his chair. He told them of the school in Paris, the distinguished visitor, the offer of the chair of Ancient Languages at Miami University, the salary of $600. He turned to his mother. "I felt I could not accept or refuse until I had my family's counsel."

The family thought the offer too good to pass up. Only Anna demurred. "You say the teachers and the president are ordained Presbyterian ministers?"

William assured her they were.

She thought a moment. "I suppose there must always be a beginning, but promise me one thing, William, if the opportunity to be ordained comes to you, that you will be ordained."

"I give you my word, Ma."

During William's stay, Anna turned over Alec's lessons to him. The boy had a new slate of which he was very proud. Having difficulty with an arithmetic problem during one lesson period, he held the slate up for William to see his work and asked for help. William tried with suggestions and leads to get him to discover the solution himself.

Alec interrupted. "Don't bother with all that, William. Just tell me, do I multiply, divide, add, or subtract."

"Alex-and-er" William rebuked, "that is not the way to learn. The object of education is learning to think. Think, boy, think!"

Alec banged the slate down on the table so hard that it cracked all the way across. Tearfully, he jumped up and ran outdoors.

"The boy is spoiled," said Anna. "He must be punished for his impatience."

"I think not, Ma. The broken slate is punishment enough." A sudden inspiration came to William. "When I return to Oxford, why don't you let me take Alec? I'm told the university has a good preparatory school."

William was surprised when his mother agreed to the plan. It wasn't like her to give over a son so young. He noticed for the first time how pale she looked, the lines in her face, the droop to her shoulders. "You work too hard, Ma. Do you not feel well?"

"It's good to be busy," she said and talked of other things. Afterward he remembered she did not answer his question about not feeling well.

Alec could hardly believe his good luck. Always before when William left he had begged to go along, and always he had been refused. This time he hadn't even asked, and—he was going

The morning of their departure William and Alec saddled their horses at the stable and rode to the cabin stoop where the family waited. William sat very tall in the saddle in his new stovepipe hat, while Alec's feet didn't reach the stirrups. William dismounted and bid each member around the circle a personal good-bye. Last of all he took his mother in his arms. How small she seemed to him now.

Impatient to be off, Alec included the family in one sweeping farewell. Then leaning from the saddle he gave his mother a hearty smack on the cheek.

Anna smiled through tears. She patted his double-stockinged leg. "Be a good boy. Mind William."

Before the dip in the road shut Gravel Hill from sight, William and Alec reined their horses, turned in their saddles, and waved a last good-bye to the small shawled figure under the silver maple.

CHAPTER SIX

Bachelorized?

Three hundred miles of raw winter travel lay behind the horseback riders as they splashed through a creek, its banks marked with crumbling blue stone, and climbed the rounded crest of a wooded hill. The road soon led out of dense forest into a clearing—and there before them stood Miami, the university buried in a western wilderness. The three-story whitewashed brick building, with west wing and cupola, occupied a campus of stumps enclosed by a whitewashed fence.

William and Alec jogged along to the south gate, dismounted, and tied their horses to the hitching rack. Together they walked up the path, bordered by a double row of winter-bare spindly poplars, to the university's main entrance. Alec would wait outside and explore the campus. As William opened the heavy oak door, he had the feeling that when he stepped across its threshold he would be stepping over the dividing line between his past and his future.

President Bishop clasped his hand warmly. "Sit down, sit down, McGuffey. So glad to see you." They talked of generalities, weather, health, William's trip, and then of the particular business at hand. He gave William a calendar of the school's daily program. From the rising bell at 5:00 a.m., study periods and classes alternated—with very brief periods out for meals and recreation—until evening prayers. Friday was the exception, as Friday afternoons were set apart for declamation and original essays and Friday evenings for debate. "We have some lively debates," the president told him, "especially those involving the question of slavery and states rights. Miami draws students from both the South and the North."

President Bishop took William on a tour of the building. He saw the first-floor chapel where he would take his turn with other faculty members preaching on Sunday, his classroom in the southwest corner of second floor, and the library where he would preside as the university's first librarian. A hall separated classrooms from student lodging. William expressed his pleasure with all that he'd seen, and thanked the president for his personal attention.

Outside, he found Alec surrounded by students at the school's well. Although they were drawing water from the open well with rope and bucket, he had a hunch they were also pumping Alec with questions about the new professor. He soon realized that if they were, the pump must have had dual action, for Alec was bubbling with information.

"William, did you know the university is built on a leveled Indian mound and the bricks are made from the clay of the mound? And there's no bell in the cupola. A student blows a bugle to call classes. The president thinks a bell would be a sinful extravagance. Do you think so, William?"

"Well, that would depend. If a school needed other things, say books . . ."

Alec tugged at William's sleeve. " 'Fore we get around the corner, William, see that path? No, not the one that goes past the school—it's the path to the privy in the woods—but the one that runs slantwise to the corner of the fence, 'Slant Walk,' the boy called it. Well, it joins up with the main street of town.

Fancy being so close to town. And the creek we crossed, it's called Four Mile Creek. You remember the blue stone in its banks, William? The stone's full of fossils. Can I—may I go back there and dig for fossils?"

"Sometime, but now we must get settled in our room." It appeared that Alec was as much taken with the place as his big brother.

They mounted their horses and followed the fence around to the corner where Slant Walk joined the street and continued along Oxford's main thoroughfare. The sight that met William's eyes shocked him out of his first pleasant reaction to the university. It wasn't the cow that lay peacefully chewing her cud in front of the tannery that processed the skins of her relatives. It wasn't the pigs that wallowed in a mud hole in the street, nor the geese that scattered noisily before the horses' hoofs. It was the count of three saloons in so small a town. And even the grocery stores advertised hard liquor. Why, the place was like a rat-trap baited for students, with Slant Walk funneling them in.

William and Alec rode on down the street to the corner opposite the town square, where above a place of business President Bishop said they would find a suitable room. Alec promptly forgot about fossils, for on the town square the weekend market was in full swing. Farmers had driven to town with loads of pumpkins, potatoes, and cabbages. Vendors hawked their wares: brooms, ax-helves, medicinal herbs. Shawled housewives sold baked goods, butter, and cheese.

That night, after their saddlebags were unpacked and Alec finally asleep, William paced the town's noisy street. Men who had imbibed too much grog staggered along singing raucous songs. A fight was going on at one of the saloons. The combined singing, fighting, and cursing made the night hideous. Never would his mother have consented to his bringing Alec into an influence like this, nor would he have suggested the idea had he known. He wandered over to the town square, empty since sunset, and sat down on a bench.

An elderly man carrying a lantern stopped by. "Stranger, be you?"

William replied that he was, and shifted position to make room on the bench. His visitor proved to be a Scotch-Irish small-farm man who grew broom corn in the summer. During the winter he made this into brooms which he sold at the market. "The profit is small," he said, "but you know the old saying, 'Many a mickle makes a muckle'."

The conversation shifted from brooms to the populace of the town. "'Tis a riffraff bunch 'ceptin the university folks and a few other families," said the man. "The land around Oxford," he explained, "could originally be had without down payment or proof of security, and such an arrangement always brings a crowd of no-accounts to the frontier." He assured William that conditions were better during the week, that weekends were the worst.

When William expressed a wish that the undesirables could somehow be removed, his bench mate told him he sounded like Reverend Porter who offered the prayer at the university's inauguration services the previous spring. "'Twas a foolish prayer," he said.

"Why do you call it foolish?" William asked.

"Faith," said the old man, "and I think it was the foolishest prayer I ever heard in me life. Why, he prayed that the Lord would move all the riffraff population from Oxford Township, and fill it wi' a good population. He might better have prayed the Lord to convert them on the ground, and save the movin'."

William's laugh helped to clear his depression. "Thank you, friend. I'll be remembering your advice when I preach in the chapel." With an invitation to attend services, he bade the maker of brooms good night.

Monday morning, William, dressed in his new black bombazine suit and carrying his equally new cane, walked with Alec along Slant Walk for his first day of teaching at Miami. To a hand accustomed to ax handle, and a body to homespun, the cane and suit felt strange, unsure. But once behind his classroom lectern with students before him, all strangeness and uncertainty left him. Taking his spectacles from his pocket, he said as he adjusted bows behind ears, "A certain man once walked a considerable distance to try my spectacles."

"Why do you wish to try spectacles?" I asked. "Are there not reading spectacles nearer your home?"

"None that reads Hebrew," the man said, "and I have a hankering to know how the Bible reads in Hebrew."

Of course, everyone laughed at the absurdity of it. But the anecdote illustrated a saying that pupils in William's classes were bound to hear again and again: No excellence without great labor.

William often used humor in his teaching. Why then was he adamant, even to the expulsion of students, against "levity," as he termed joking. If asked, he would explain that the kind of humor that made a point or advanced the topic under discussion was acceptable, but students' jokes, for the most part, were made to draw attention to themselves and to divert attention from the recitation. But in spite of strict discipline that sometimes earned him the title, "Guff the Terrible," his classes were always full and his church services crowded.

January went by quickly, filled to the brim with activity—teaching, preaching, tutoring Alec, coaching students. Rumor had soon spread that Professor McGuffey was not only a willing critic, but a first-class critic of declamation. An entry in a student's diary reads, "I have an appointment with Professor McGuffey at five o'clock tomorrow morning for help on my Friday's piece."

Meanwhile, Alec was proving William's theory that a foreign language is acquired faster when young. William had enrolled him in the Hebrew grammar class, and though he started late he was climbing toward the top of the class. The white fence was his boundary limit toward town. His pockets often bulged with fossils. Combed and scrubbed, he accompanied William to neighboring churches and faculty teas. Champion tree climber and broad jumper among boys of his age, and good even in fisticuffs, at tea parties he was the proper gentleman, fussed over by hostesses. Alec adored tea parties.

Mail arrived once a week in Oxford by post rider. With each mail delivery William looked for a letter postmarked Washington, Pennsylvania, and addressed in a firm masculine hand. Did Professor Wylie not approve of his coming to Oxford? Miami trustees would be meeting in March, and he expected a formal invitation to fill the chair of Ancient Languages, which he now filled temporarily. His family had given its approval, but he coveted assurance from friend Wylie. Besides, he wanted to know what he could do to earn his diploma.

February brought the long-awaited letter. Eagerly he broke the seal. The first part of the missive recounted news of the Wylie family and school events. Then followed the answer to his query: "I do not anticipate the least difficulty," wrote the president of Washington College, "of procuring for you an AB in the spring. I did wish you to remain and graduate with us and afterward settle in some situation within striking distance of me. I am inclined to think you acted wisely in going to Oxford. You had raked up all the information to be found here and the prospect afforded you there of being useful and the same time preparing for more extended usefulness . . ."

William read on to the complimentary close. He reread the letter. How he wished he could grip the hand that wrote it. An A.B. (*Artium Baccalaureatus*) in the spring was more than he had dared hope for. This was a college degree given to students who studied the Classics: Greek, Latin, and Classical Civilization as well as the liberal arts and sciences.

He must write his mother. Had she not had the faith, he would never have made it. "More extended usefulness," Wylie held out as a goal. He would do his best to achieve it. His pleasant thoughts were suddenly interrupted by a terrific crash on Miami's roof. Brick and mortar hailed down past the front window. He rushed to the side window and threw it open. "Don't jump, McGuffey!" called a workman from below. "It's only the cupola that's collapsed."

In April, William and John Annan, the mathematics teacher, covered Butler County on horseback recruiting students. Their travel took them on a network of old Indian trails and along the dusty banks of the new canal which, when completed, would connect Lake Erie by river route with the Ohio. A similar canal was under construction in the eastern part of the state. The canals, it was estimated, would increase the value of Ohio's produce from five to 10 times. Instead of three cents a pound for butter and four cents a dozen for eggs, Ma would get 15 and 20 cents. Pa would find a ready market for his corn. All Ohio would prosper. Student enrollment would double at Miami.

William and John Annan returned to Oxford with a cavalcade of students that they put to work removing stumps from the college campus. Boys from the backwoods worked in respectful awe of the professor from up north. If he could teach Greek and Latin as well as he could sling an ax, he ought to be good!

In June, William received the A.B. degree. J. W. Scott, secretary of the board of trustees, and a former teacher of William's wrote an accompanying letter:

"Permit my most sincere congratulations to Professor McGuffey. I presume he will not now demure to my addressing him by that

title. At the last meeting of the Board we had the subject of granting you a diploma brought forward. There appeared to be perfect
concurrence of sentiment with respect to granting it." Then followed some personal news in which he stated his wife had presented him with a new daughter. "I suppose though your feelings
have become so bachelorized that you can scarcely realize my
pleasure. What do you think on the subject of matrimony? Do
you think it possible to love any woman as well as Latin or
Greek?"

William laid the letter down with mixed feelings. The unanimous vote of the board in granting the diploma filled him with
humble gratitude. But that last part of the letter—had he become bachelorized to the extent Scott suggested? Would there
never be a woman in his life other than his mother? Children?
He loved children.

It would seem from what happened shortly after receiving the
letter that its direct questions had prompted the "goddess of love"
to act. One morning as William passed the Spinning mercantile
store on his way to class he saw, framed by the store window and
its merchandise, a demure lovely face. The violet-gray eyes had
glanced at him as he passed. Had the small mouth smiled? Likely
not. All day the memory of the face had a disturbing way of in-
terposing itself as he discussed Roman antiquities or led his class
in conjugating Latin verbs. For a phantom second even Caesar
wore dark brown curls instead of laurel wreath. After session he
caught himself dawdling on the sheet of blank paper that lay before him awaiting the next day's assignment.

Characteristically, William did not long tolerate such idle day-
dreaming. As if preparing for a debate, he ushered the facts and
applied cold logic. True, he had glimpsed the most lovely face
he had ever seen. The face belonged to a young lady arranging
merchandise in the Spinning store window. He knew nothing
about her, not even her name. And common sense told him that

one so beautiful would not look the second time at one so admittedly homely as he. He coerced the dawdling quill into preparing an outline of tomorrow's lecture on the Acropolis of Athens.

But for once William's analytical mind failed to resolve the question correctly. At a party given by Charles Spinning, William met the young lady whose "demure lovely face" had disturbed his classes and distorted Caesar. She proved to be the merchant's sister, Harriet Elliott Spinning of Dayton, Ohio. And the young lady did look at him the second time, in fact, the third, fourth, and fifth times.

Spring brought a round of tea parties. Hostesses began to pair William and Harriet on their lists of guests. Over cups of tea the couple learned each other's background. William recounted anecdotes of Gravel Hill, and Harriet told of Woodside, the farm near Dayton where she had grown up. With both pride and sadness she spoke of her father, Judge Isaac Spinning, who had been one of the first associate judges of Ohio, and who had died just the previous December. Now that both parents were deceased she had come to stay for a time with Charles, the next oldest of her three brothers.

The humid hot summer of southern Ohio simmered by. Young folk defeated the heat by early morning canters in the woods and picnic suppers under the drowsy eucalyptus of Four Mile Creek—Tallawanda, the Indians called the stream. Alec and his friends spent hours swimming, splashing, and ducking each other in the creek's several swimming holes. Alec sort of felt he had priority rights. Hadn't General Anthony Wayne named the creek Four Mile, it being the fourth stream his army crossed when marching north to fight the Indians? And wasn't Pa one of the army's foremost scouts? Alec figured Pa had waded the creek ahead of the army, and well, didn't that give him some sort of first rights?

In the fall Charles Spinning gave up his Oxford business to look after the Woodside farm at Dayton and of course Harriet went with him. Before her departure William figured out a way to thwart the conventions of correspondence and at the same time observe them. Convention decreed that a young man, when writing to a young lady, address his letters to her father or guardian. "I shall address my letters to your brother," confided William, "but I shall underline the middle initial."

Gray eyes sparkled with conspiracy. "And I shall meet the post carrier," said Harriet.

Never had William missed anyone as he missed Harriet. The picture of a future with Harriet by his side grew more desirable every day. He felt a great urge to counsel with Andrew Wylie about things marital, and decided to write. Not yet ready to admit a serious friendship, he wrote of school routine, the western trek of pioneers through Oxford, and just casually asked Wylie's advice concerning matrimony.

On the last day of January came the reply. A good correspondent, Wylie tossed back the conversational ball, paragraph for paragraph, including the one on matrimony:

"No man, or woman either, ever yet asked advice about matrimony till resolved to commit it. Whoever she is I wish Cupid, and Venus, and Romula—may be present at the wedding."

The first day of spring vacation William jounced over the rutted road to Dayton with horse and rented carriage. On April 3, 1827, he and Harriet exchanged marriage vows in the parlor at Woodside.

No groom ever took the vow to "love, honor, and cherish" more seriously than did William. His wife should never know the drudgery of work as had his mother. So thinking he arranged for both lodging and board for his family—Alec was thrilled with the new sister-in-law—at the only brick house in Oxford. There Harriet would be free to do all those feminine things he imagined a woman was wont to do if she had the opportunity. He arranged for the painting of her portrait.

William plunged into his work, goaded with renewed vigor by the added pleasurable responsibility. Evenings, he coached Alec, who attended grammar school during the day, in Greek and Latin. Latin had become a recreation between the brothers. If Harriet looked on wistfully, William did not notice. If Harriet sighed as she munched the cookie served her with the evening cup of tea, he most likely would inquire, "Have you had a hard day, my dear?" He never dreamed that a longing to bake cookies instead of consuming them, a desire to wait on someone instead of being waited on, had caused the sigh.

Anna wrote asking when did William plan to bring his bride home for a visit. He replied probably the next spring. But when next spring came, he wrote that Harriet was not strong enough to stand the trip. In fact, he was frankly worried. She had lost weight. Her cheeks had become pallid. She had little energy. He was taking her to the local physician for consultation.

Dr. Hughes, nephew of the principal of Old Stone Academy, gave William a jolt when he told him that Harriet was suffering from an overdose of coddling on his part. That as a plant protected from the rigors of sun, rain, and wind became pale and spindly so did the human body. Give his wife the interest of a home to run, responsibilities to share, sunshine and fresh air, and he would soon see improvement.

Acting on the physician's advice, William purchased four acres of land with a weathered frame house on Spring Street opposite the university campus. He had but to look up from his classroom desk to see the house. The day Aunt Prue, who had been the Spinning children's mammy, came from Dayton to join the family, they moved into their new home. Aunt Prue took one look at her former charge and said, "Law me chile, you needs to work in the garden, and to get you some chillun."

Evenings now, the McGuffeys studied plans for a new two-story brick house to be built in front of and adjoining the frame house. They would build as they were financially able. With careful saving—William's salary had been materially increased—they figured they could complete their home within three years. There would be six rooms, a parlor with portico entrance, a dining room, and kitchen on the main floor. A narrow stair would lead to sleeping rooms on the second floor. Harriet's delight was a two-story enclosed east veranda.

That Harriet might have the benefit of more fresh air and sunshine, William purchased a buggy and a driving horse named Charley. Now Harriet as well as Alec could accompany him to nearby churches where he preached when it was not his turn to hold Sunday service in the college chapel. But not all country congregations were prepared for the sight of a spanking new buggy among the wagons and saddle horses lining the hitching racks of their meeting houses, especially when it belonged to the preacher, who, according to tradition, should be both pious and penurious.

The elders at Garrtown detained William in the churchyard after service. "Professor McGuffey, we like your preaching," said the spokesman, "but we don't like your being so stylish."

"Stylish?" William questioned.

"You wear a silk coat," the man explained, "and you keep a fine horse and carriage."

"I keep a horse and carriage," admitted William, "so that my wife who is not strong can be out in the fresh air and also attend services with me. As to my coat, examine it, gentlemen. It is of shiny material but not silk. I dare say each of you has two coats. I have only one."

The elders apologized. But the spring day projected yet another sour note which the sweetish fragrance of locust trees in bloom could not counteract.

A second service, held by a farmer preacher of another denomination, had already begun as Alec untied Charley. The preacher's opening remarks floated clearly out of the open church windows to the three at the buggy. "I thank the Lord I have never rubbed my back again a college wall. Now if I say anything good, it comes hot from heaven."

A pained expression crossed Harriet's face. Alec gave a vicious yank on the dashboard as he climbed into the buggy. William smiled ruefully. "Never mind," he consoled. "Education will bring about a change of thinking even in Garrtown. Education changes attitudes."

The long weekend rides into the country and the stimulus of planning the new home while supervising the old brought marked improvement to Harriet's health. Color came back into her cheeks, sparkle to her eyes. William promised his mother that the next spring as soon as swollen freshets receded so they could ford the streams, Harriet, Alec, and he would ride home for a visit.

But streams were far from the spring freshet stage, their voices still locked with January's ice and snow, when a telegram arrived from Gravel Hill: "Ma dangerously ill. Come at once." It was then that William recalled his mother hadn't answered his question about not feeling well.

Hurriedly arranging for his classes and the comfort of Harriet and Aunt Prue, William and Alec caught up the saddle horses and began the 300-mile trek to Gravel Hill. They lengthened the short winter days by keeping to the trail long after the stars had lit the sky, and resuming it before the sun snuffed them out. They defeated the cold and saved their horses' strength by often jogging along beside the animals. Finally they reached Youngstown and turned into the McGuffey Road. Its last incline brought the leafless silver maple into view. Had it been three years since Ma, a shawled figure, stood there waving good-bye?

They soon found they had come too late for her final good-bye, but were consoled to know she had included them. Unconsciousness had claimed her. With Pa, Henry sat at the bedside, his sensitive doctor's fingers on her slowing pulse. He had done all he could. The tearful family stood at the foot of the bed, the bed cleated to the corner of the cabin in which all but the three eldest had been born.

As they waited for the end, William felt a slender boyish hand slip uncertainly into his. He closed his palm reassuringly over it. The moment marked the beginning of a pact between the eldest and the youngest McGuffey brothers—what's mine is yours to share. After the burial service in the New Bedford Cemetery, William and Alec retraced the road they had so recently traveled, the long journey back to Harriet and the weathered frame house on Spring Street in Oxford.

CHAPTER SEVEN

No Thought of Fame, Less of Fortune

A proverb? A parable? Tomorrow would be William's turn to occupy the chapel pulpit but a key text evaded him. As he thumbed through the book of Proverbs and the Gospel According to St. Matthew, the sound of harness bells lured his attention outside the classroom window. And the sight out there tempted him into a reminiscence that had nothing to do with neither proverbs, parables, or tomorrow's chapel sermon.

Brass bells jangled energetically from harnesses, quite in contrast to the plodding six horses that pulled a swaying Conestoga wagon along the dusty road in front of Miami's campus. Under the arch of tow cloth a sunbonneted woman holding a baby sat beside the swarthy driver, a small boy between them. No telling how many more children rode under the canopy with farm implements, chests, featherbeds, trunks, pots, and piggins. Books? Probably the family Bible and possibly a Webster's speller. A string of farm animals stretched out behind the wagon. Boys on horseback kept them moving. The last rider was still visible through a haze of dust when a double yoke of oxen pulling a farm wagon lumbered out of the woods to the east. Since early fall the road, once an Indian trail to the Kentucky hunting grounds, had become a continuous line of emigrants moving westward.

91

The wagons, William knew, carried families of various nationalities—German, Scotch, Swedish, Polish, English—some directly from overseas, others from Kentucky and the states east of the Alleghenies. He knew that at the end of the journey they would settle in communities and eventually build schools. And he knew exactly what those schools would be like. He had taught in them when Ohio was more or less the end of the road west. The only difference would be in building material, for these would be of sod instead of log.

Children would walk miles to attend a three-months' term taught by a roving teacher, sometimes qualified but more not. William visualized the greased-paper windows, the backless benches, the few dog-eared books. German youngsters would pronounce W's as V's and vice versa: "Ve vill vork very goot." Small Huidrich would boast, "Mine dog can run the hill up. Nein?" Young Scots would say "ye ken" for you know, "canna" for cannot. Backwoods children would caution teacher to take "keer" when he went home "cuz the crik aire runnin' plumb full." Dialect, brogue, and distorted English would meet in the one-room schools. There would be differences in manners and morals and a slowness to shift loyalties from their own unique ethnic group to encompass and accept others who were not just like themselves.

What common denominator—weren't the children small fractions of the expanding West—would best blend their speech into correct English, expand their knowledge, and at the same time develop a code of good citizenship and a patriotism for America? A series of suitable readers, William was convinced, could accomplish all four objectives. He had just written a book, *Treatise on Methods of Reading*, which would be published by a London firm. It had grown out of his experience in coaching elocution students. Perhaps by the time the how-to-teach-reading book came out, someone would have published a set of readers on grammar school level to supplement its instruction.

So engrossed was William in his thinking that he barely heard the purposeful knock on his door. He opened it to a woman of imposing appearance who said she must speak with him about an important matter. William offered her a chair.

His visitor adjusted an eyeglass and plunged into her subject without preliminaries. "I have come to discuss the problem of children."

"I, too," said William, "have been thinking of the problems of children."

Not noticing, or ignoring the difference between "the problem of children," and the "problems of children," the woman continued. "I have a biblical reference, a key text that definitely settles the problem of children's attendance at meetings."

"This is truly a coincidence. Before you came to call I was not only thinking of children but also pondering a key text for my tomorrow's sermon. What is your text, Madam?"

"In 1 Samuel 6:7 we are told that the calves were not allowed to accompany the cow mothers that pulled the cart on which rested the holy ark. It reads, 'Bring their calves home from them.' Home! That's where the children belong!"

The woman leaned forward, content that this text plainly teaches that small children should not accompany their mothers to church where the Holy Scriptures are expounded. "The children get no good out of the service and they bother those who would," she concluded.

"In what way do children bother you, my friend?"

"They wiggle."

William's explosive cough required a kerchief. "I shall preach on the subject of children and church attendance tomorrow. I think it will be good for all of us.

The woman arose. "Thank you, Professor McGuffey. Make it strong."

"I shall make it strong," William assured his guest as he saw her to the door.

The black silk voluminous skirt rustled down the hall. Its corded hemline reached the floor and gave the illusion that the skirt propelled itself along, the wearer riding atop its billowy folds.

When William mounted the pulpit at 11:00 o'clock the next morning, the chapel was well filled. Reverently he turned the pages of the pulpit Bible and then paused. In the hush that followed, he read the key text of his sermon: "Suffer little children to come unto me and forbid them not." If he stressed the word "little" it was due to an inner prompting to make the meaning clear to a certain listener, but he fought against being antagonistic.

In a conversational style—seldom did William resort to the ministerial tune and never to the hellfire harangue popular in that day—he enlarged on the text, picturing a mountainside where lilies bloomed and where sat the Teacher of Teachers surrounded by adults. He told of the disciples' rebuke to some mothers who had presumed to bring their children. He spoke of the Great Teacher's instruction to let the children come to Him, the adults making way. William spoke with conviction and warmth. For him the subject was not only rooted in Scripture but in sentiment as well. He would always remember the first Sunday after the completion of the McGuffey Road when his whole family piled into the new wagon and Pa drove them to Reverend Wick's cabin in Youngstown for church service. Ma had looked forward to that day during 10 long, churchless years.

William closed his sermon with a scriptural climax, "Except ye . . . become as little children ye shall not enter the kingdom of heaven." He took his place at the chapel door to shake hands as the congregation filed out. "Excellent sermon" . . . "Good advice" . . . "Guess we'd best set more store by the young'uns" commented parishioners.

What of his visitor of the day before? Was she convinced?

The billowy skirt floated out of the chapel door without so much as a pause for its wearer to shake hands.

Contention seemed to be in the air. Perhaps it was the feel of fall attempting to stave off winter that cast an influence on humans. At any rate, the Universalists challenged William to a debate. They purposed to show the superiority of liberal Universalism over conservative Presbyterianism. Why had they picked on him? Were they irked because he preached in all the churches round about, or did they consider a young professor not yet ordained an easy prey?

Miami's debating teams crowded the place of debate to witness their coach in action. He had drilled into them, "Reflect on both sides of the question. Write down your thoughts, but never take the paper to the debate, nor try to remember the words you have written . . . better words will come with the stimulus of combat." Now they would see his instruction put to the test.

Some of the students held prejudices favoring the liberal side, but loyalty outweighed prejudice. They would stand behind Guff. However, it soon became apparent that Guff, single-handed, was more than a match for his multiple foe. His points, logical and lucid, built up to an irrefutable climax. A dry humor carried the rebuttal to victory.

Miami's debaters were jubilant. They would gladly have toted the victor home, but Guff just wasn't the type. In some respects, the enthusiastic promoter of debate arid elocution was a mite disappointing. After the contest he shook hands with his challengers, shrugged off laurels, and hurried home to draft an article on education for the *Western Monthly* magazine. One of the "liberals," Charlie Anderson (who later became governor of Kentucky), summed up the debate for the Miami *Bulletin*: "William McGuffey," he wrote, "left his adversaries no room for even a claim of victory."

The year 1830 brought two major experiences to the McGuffeys. On January 20, a baby girl was born. They named her Mary Haines. She was a healthy, strong, bouncy child. William always maintained she should have been a boy, but always added that she made a pretty fine girl.

On October 8, with Indian summer mixing a heady fragrance of wild grapes and the wood smoke of clearings, the McGuffeys drove along Indian Creek to Bethel, a small brick Presbyterian church. Faculty, friends, and theology students occupied the pews. They had come to attend William's ordination. Reverend Thomas Thomas preached the sermon, Reverend Robert Bishop delivered the charge to the people. Harriet and Alec sat in a front pew. How William wished that his mother were sitting there beside them. His ordination fulfilled his last promise to her.

March brought a letter addressed in an unfamiliar hand and postmarked West Middleton, Virginia. Puzzled, William broke the wax seal and straightened the single page. The missive read:

"My dear Friend,

"I send you this note to let you know that two weeks ago today I had the pleasure of solemnizing your father's second marriage to a widow Dickey, a member of my congregation. She has been a widow about nine years. During this time she conducted herself with great prudence and I think her a valuable lady . . . William Wallace"

So Pa had remarried. How strange it would seem to visit Gravel Hill and find a new woman's presence dominating the familiar log cabin, sitting in Ma's rocker before the fireplace, knitting socks on the bench under the silver maple. How hard it must be for a man or woman who had lived long years with another mate to make the adjustment to a new partner. He didn't believe he—

As quick as it came, the thought was rejected.

William was not surprised that Pa had not written. Since Ma's death the girls had cared for his correspondence, and the Reverend Wallace had mentioned that the new wife could not write. In Anna's last letter she had written that Pa was spending the winter with relatives in Pennsylvania and Virginia. There, evidently, he had found a wife. It was better that he marry, William pondered. A man needed a home of his own rather than to live with his children. He made a wry face. And this time Pa had selected a mate that wouldn't be insisting that sons go away to college!

The *Treatise on Methods of Reading* had been off the press for some months. He found it a boon in teaching college students. But as yet no magic set of reading books had appeared to supplement it in grammar schools. "At that level," he told Harriet, "it's an example of hitching the cart before the horse."

Then came the day he received an advance copy of a reader that was advertised as America's First Reader. Splendid! At last those children attending the one-room schools, now numbering more than a million, would be supplied with readers. The book was said to be the first of a set of three. Eagerly William opened the reader, designed for America's youngest, to the table of contents, and read:

Filial Sensibility
Noble Behavior of Scipio
Virtue in Humble Life
The Female Choice
Ingratitude to Our Supreme Benefactor, Highly Culpable

With that abstract rhetorical title he slammed the book shut. What did people think children were? Miniature adults with the only reason for existence of some day being six feet instead of three? Couldn't grown-ups remember how it felt to be a child with a curiosity that asked how polliwogs became toads, how flies walked on the ceiling? Had they forgotten the thrill of running in the meadow with a kite at the end of a string, of teaching a dog to fetch a stick or to "speak" for a tidbit? It seemed so.

Morals were excellent. He believed a story without a lesson was a story without a purpose, like a coat that had looks but no warmth. But a moral need not make a story dull. What could be more exciting than Aesop's "The Lion and the Mouse" or "The Hare and the Tortoise?" But too much moral and too little story or no story . . .

The longer William pondered the reader situation the more in-censed he became. Readers were the answer to a unified language in the West, to a unified code of good citizenship—he saw it so clearly. But readers should be fun! They should be informative. They should contain the best in literature. His eyes narrowed to purposeful slits. He would compile a set of readers himself!

With no thought of fame, and less of fortune, and no assur-ance that his readers would ever be published, he set to work. He ordered a table built, an octagonal table of dining room size with a sloping lazy Susan top. "Build it of cherry wood," he told cabinetmaker Murrell, "and in each of its eight sides make a pie-shaped drawer that glides easily."

When finished, the table almost filled the study in the old frame house. Had it required a name, it could well have been designated the Good Citizenship Table, with drawers labeled kindness, in-dustry, honesty, courage, thrift, and the like. Out of an old trunk stored in the attic William brought his much used and now musty reading folders, relics of his roving teacher days. He made a col-lection of available readers, most of them compiled by headmas-ters of private schools for "the gifted of the better families," and others by overseas authors with an overseas background. He began sorting stories and poems from his folders, selecting other stories and poems from books, revising those that did not fit the more rural West, and writing others from experience.

The "kindness" drawer soon filled with stories of kindness to animals, playmates, the poor, and the sick. Henry's rescue of Old Blue, titled "The Kind Boy," found a place in the drawer. So did the story of "The Lame Dog," in which a man put a splint on a stray dog's injured leg, fed him, and sent him on his way. A week later the dog returned bringing a lame dog with him, as if to say, "You made my leg well, now pray do the same for this poor dog."

Sometimes the kindness was by animals toward humans, as in "Peter Pindar's Story." In it a dog rescued a half-frozen little boy from a snowdrift. And then there was "Faithful Frisk." The jam-smeared, frayed story sheet suggested that "cross-eyed, feather-tailed" Frisk had been a favorite with young pupils. On the morning of pear-picking day, so the story claimed, Harry, who was to have been high-climber, teased the little dog unmercifully, cut the curls from Annie's doll, and broke grandmother's spectacles. His conduct being "inordinately off" he was sent to bed for the entire day.

Lonely, he could hear the fun outside. How he wished for a pear! Then came a pit-a-pat on the stair. Hesitantly the bedroom door pushed open. In came Frisk with a pear in his mouth. He bounded onto the bed, gave Harry the pear, and kept him company the long afternoon.

Along with kindness William rated industry. Into this drawer went "Hugh Idle and Mr. Toil," "Frank and the Hour Glass," and the favorite old fable, "The Lark and the Farmer." A lark had a nest of young in a field of maize that ripened before her young were fledged. When the farmer sent for his neighbors to reap the corn, the terrified brood begged their mother to move them.

"Mark my word, children," said the lark, "there is no danger so long as the farmer depends on his neighbors to do his work."

But when the neighbors did not respond, and neither did his kinsmen, the farmer decided to reap the field himself. "Now, my dears," said the lark, "we must indeed be gone. For when a man resolves to do his own work, mark my word, it will be done."

And so the stories in the pie-shaped drawers multiplied: animal stories, play stories, work stories, Indian stories, Bible stories, and poems. Though in many of the stories the children were exemplary, by no means were they all goody-goodies. Boys plagued girls, drowned cats, deceived neighbors, and girls pouted, meddled, and ate too much. They represented a cross section of the boys and girls William had taught in the one-room schools.

Always aware of the neglected smaller children who often spent a whole term chanting ABC's and identifying them in words, followed by another term of spelling, nothing but spelling—William determined to put readers into their hands from the very first. They'd start with a pictorial primer, and out of the reading would grow spelling. Alec, now 15, and a freshman in the university, became interested in developing spelling lessons to coincide with the reading lessons. Harriet's interest centered in the primer, influenced no doubt by the fact that Mary Haines had reached the inquiring age of 2.

It was spring in Oxford, cold and wet, but spring nevertheless, when the McGuffeys, now numbering five—as baby Henrietta, "Henny" to her father, had joined the family circle the previous summer—moved into the new brick addition to their home. The ember-red paint of the exterior did its best to moderate the day's chill. The six fireplaces, one in each room, banished it entirely from the interior. William initiated the move by installing Harriet's portrait over the parlor mantel. The hostess thus presiding, the room took on the appearance of at-homeness as carpet, lace curtains, black horsehair sofa, oak rockers, and footstools were added.

The dining room puzzled strangers, not because of its olive green walls bordered with stencil of deeper green, nor the built-in glass cupboards, nor the buffet displaying a blue willow soup tureen. Eyebrows lifted on seeing the regular dining table pushed to one side, while rows of low benches occupied the center of the room. Rather than satisfy a visitor's curiosity at the moment, William would invite them to return, say at 10:00 o'clock on a weekday morning.

Outside, under the parlor window next to the portico, William planted pink oleanders, Harriet's favorite flower. From the woods he transplanted sassafras and elms. He reserved the important location beside the gate for a young maple tree. The choice of maple could well have been prompted by the memory of the silver maple at Gravel Hill, a sort of memorial to his mother. Now that house and grounds were finished he began an experiment, the first of its kind, ever to be tried in America.

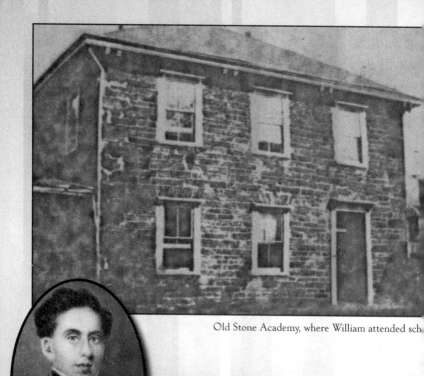

Old Stone Academy, where William attended sch

Alexander "Alec"
McGuffey at age 17.
He helped his brother
develop the six-edition
McGuffey Eclectic Readers.

Harriet Spinning McGuffey,
William's first wife, whose
face "disturbed William's
classes"

Laura Howard McGuffey
(William called his second
wife "Lura") was the daught
of the dean of the medical
college at the University of
Virginia.

The octagonal table on which the McGuffey Readers were written. The table is in its original place in the McGuffey home. The writing desk against the wall features a sloping top and eight drawers for storing manuscripts.

First editions of the McGuffey Readers (now collectors' items)

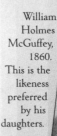

William Holmes McGuffey, 1860. This is the likeness preferred by his daughters.

The red brick house the McGuffeys built on Spring Street, Oxford, Ohio (now the McGuffey Museum). The original portico was later extended across the front.

150 (later 58) Main Street, Cincinnati, Ohio, where the McGuffey Readers were first published

The first cover of *Eclectic Primer*, 1837 (first edition printed with yellow paper cover and priced at eight cents).

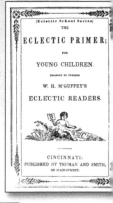

Title page and illustrations in *First Reader* (edition printed in 1844, priced at 10 cents)

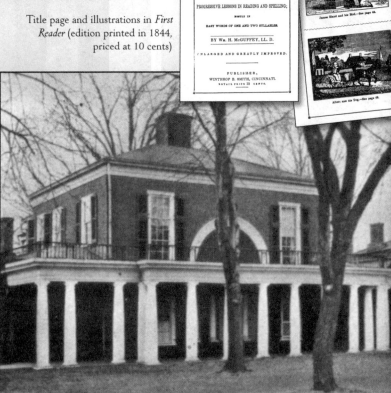

Pavilion No. 9, McGuffey's home at the University of Virginia

McGuffey ash, one of the trees he planted (Virginia)

McGuffey statue (lower part): Miami University, Oxford, Ohio

McGuffey monument: Miami University, Oxford, Ohio

Tombstone of William McGuffey, University of Virginia Cemetery. (Lura's grave is to the left.)

CHAPTER EIGHT

The Knuckle Whistle School

The new bell in the cupola clanged 10:00 o'clock, and Professor McGuffey had a vacant period. With long strides that still hinted of a woodsman's background he crossed the campus toward the red brick house on the corner of Spring Street. At the picket gate he turned, placed cupped hands to his mouth, and blew a knuckle whistle blast.

Doors burst open, and like jacks-in-a-box, children popped out. Girls in white pinafores over pink and blue dresses, boys in trousers and ruffled shirts—they had been waiting for the signal—ran toward the man at the gate. Jane, Elizabeth, Ebenezer, George, Christine . . . when all were accounted for the troop, led by the six-foot captain, marched along the cinder path to the east side of the house and entered through the veranda door. Into the dining room they filed and took their places on the low benches.

Now the bench puzzle offered its own solution. School took over. Out came the reader manuscripts. Children, themselves, would be the final judges of reader interest and reading difficulty of the stories that would find their way into the McGuffey Readers. On warm days the class met out-of-doors under the elms that bordered the garden. There, logs served as benches. All too soon the hour-and-a-half came to an end. Teacher and pupils marched back to the gate where school was dismissed until the next knuckle whistle blast.

No Miami teacher could have been busier than William McGuffey. He taught a full class load in the Mental and Moral Philosophy Department of the university. (At his insistence he had been transferred to that department the year the red brick house was completed.) He coached the students of debate and elocution, preached every Sunday, lectured in Ohio and bordering states promoting free grammar schools, and conducted the neighborhood children's training school.

Daily he noted the progress in reading skills of his pupils. "The rate of progress," he told a lecture audience, "is in direct ratio to reading interest." Boys' interests centered in stilts, kites, and skates; girls' in dolls, tea parties, and jump ropes. Both enjoyed animal stories, especially dog and horse stories. Bird stories also rated high, perhaps because of the live laboratory on top the McGuffey stable—and thereon hangs a family incident.

Remembering how the youngsters at Gravel Hill enjoyed the bluebirds, once when returning from an out-of-town lecture, William brought home a pair of pigeons as a surprise for Mary Haines and Henny. It being supper time when he arrived, and knowing the little girls would be too excited about the pigeons to eat, he left the birds in their basket, covered with a cloth, behind the hall door. Supper over, he announced, "There's a present for you children in the hall behind the door."

Mary Haines slid off her chair and eagerly disappeared into the dark hall. She soon returned, soberly shaking her head. "No present, Papa. Just kitty cat."

"The cat!" William fairly upset his chair getting to the hall. The cat was there but she hadn't yet made up her feline mind what to do about the basket of tantalizing bird smell. The next day William nailed a red chest, quite a contrast to Old Blue's hollow tree branch, to the ridgepole of the barn where the pigeons, Bob and Bell, set up housekeeping and became the chief actors in a number of reader stories.

Under William's pen, current happenings, some major, some minor, often developed into reader lessons or recalled to him a fable or poem he'd once read. Out of the dead of night came the tale of "The Seven Sticks." Aroused from a sound sleep between midnight and 1:00 a.m., William began to realize that he was not dreaming, that the voices he heard were real.

"Liberty and Union, now and forever, one and inseparable," chanted a score or more of male enthusiasts. And then in clipped staccato—"Down with states' rights! Away with slavery!"

William got up and went to the window. Along Spring Street marched a torchlight procession. Such demonstrations were not infrequent by Miami students. The topics of states' rights and slavery aroused bitter debate and dissension between students of the North and students of the South. It had even invaded the faculty. William had friends on both sides, and took little part in the arguments. Grown men seldom changed their minds. He would appeal to the children. "As the twig is bent . . ."

States' rights? Tecumseh's experience knocked at his memory. Tecumseh had argued against "tribes' rights." He had journeyed from campfire to campfire persuading tribesmen to forget tribal quarrels and unite in a great Indian empire. Had the Indians listened, who knows how long they might have held their hunting grounds. Pa claimed that "men must stand together to build a strong nation." How best could the idea be gotten across to children? Webster's oration—the marchers were chanting its closing summary—was declamation on a college level, suitable for an advanced reader.

He searched his memory for something on the level of the training school youngsters. In the distance, the torch lights of the marchers flickered like huge candles, and he recalled an old folk tale, "The Bundle of Twigs." *Just the thing,* he thought, *if told in simpler language, and the title changed to "The Seven Sticks."*

A man had seven sons who were always quarreling. One day he called his sons around him and laid before them seven sticks tied in a bundle. "I will pay a hundred dollars to the one who can break this bundle of sticks," he said.

"It can't be done," said the seven sons after each had done his best to break the bundle of sticks.

"And yet my sons nothing is easier to do." The father untied the bundle of sticks and broke them one by one.

"Anybody could do it that way," said the sons.

"As it is with these sticks, so it is with you my sons. So long as you hold fast together and aid each other, none can injure you. But if the bands of union be broken, it will happen to you just as it has to these sticks."

"Home, city, country, all are prosperous found

"When by the powerful link of union bound."

William avoided stories that smacked of church creed or dogma other than the Ten Commandments. Those million children needing readers were of many faiths. Perhaps that is why he later eliminated a story that once lay filed in the octagonal table. But the background of the story still holds.

On October the first, 1834, a son was born to the McGuffeys whom they named William Holmes. Now William had a son to carry on his name. Two-year-old Henny could hardly be persuaded to leave "Little Brother's" cradle, and she screamed with terror when Aunt Prue brought the weighing scales, a hand scale with steel hook. She had seen the hook thrust into a slab of beef when weighing it. William, always patient with this delicate, sensitive little daughter, took her on his knee and explained how babies were weighed.

Little William's weight indicated a healthy child. But the weight built false hopes. Fourteen days later the baby died.

Henny could not understand why she was suddenly barred from the nursery. Her grief-stricken father, lacking words to explain death to one so young, suggested that she and Mary Haines go for a walk in the garden. The suggestion proved to be an unfortunate one.

The girls were sitting on the veranda step when a man, carrying a small casket on his shoulder, came around the corner of the house. "They are going to put Little Brother in that box," volunteered practical Mary Haines.

Henny jumped up and slipped through the door into the house beside the man. When a neighbor woman quietly directed him to the nursery upstairs, Henny grabbed his legs with both arms and hung on. "You can't put Little Brother in that box," she screamed. "You can't!"

The neighbor had forcibly detached Henny when William came to the rescue and carried his wailing daughter into the study. What he said to comfort her can only be surmised from the story that once appeared in the reader series and was afterward deleted—a story about cocoons and butterflies, and life after death. He used Isaiah's description of the New Earth, "The wolf and the lamb shall lie down together . . . and a little child shall lead them."

A year later another baby son occupied the cradle in the nursery. The parents named him Charles Spinning after Harriet's brother, but to Henny he was Little Brother released from his coffin cocoon.

An occasional fun story found a place in the manuscripts. "The New Slate," the tale that had entertained 5-year-old Alec (Alec now attended William's alma mater, Washington College) with its comic drawings of a duck that had four legs and a pig that had two, produced giggles and laughter in the training school. Trick stories were taboo unless the trickster learned a proper lesson. One such episode that took place in the red brick house when Harriet was away, didn't so much as make it to a drawer in the octagonal table. William hadn't the heart to teach the tricksters the necessary lesson.

Harriet had been called to Dayton to lend a hand in her brother's family. She took baby Charles with her but left Mary Haines and Henny in the care of Aunt Prue. Hardly had she left the house when Miss Sarah, a neighbor spinster, carrying a satchel, rapped the McGuffey doorknocker. She brushed past Aunt Prue, and by the time William came home she had installed herself in the guest room. She informed him that she had come to see that little feet did not go astray during a mother's absence. Aunt Prue, she insisted, was too easygoing to take full charge of children; she was bound to spoil them.

William had no difficulty measuring up to men, but when it came to women, especially a strong character like Miss Sarah, he was nonplussed. So Miss Sarah stayed in spite of Aunt Prue's and Mary Haines's protests. Henny stuck close to her sister.

The first complaint that William received from Miss Sarah about his "naughty little girls" concerned something that had happened in the parlor. She had humored the children, she said, by allowing them to brush her hair. Forty strokes a day keeps the hair in condition, she informed him. Did Miss Sarah glance knowingly at his bald head? During the brushing, the mason had come to check the parlor chimney. Feeling horribly immodest with her hair down, she had attempted to flee. Could Professor McGuffey imagine her embarrassment when she found she was tied to the chair—yes, actually tied by her hair to the chair!

A new angle on the hair incident developed when William questioned the children. "We get tired of brushing Miss Sarah's hair every day," complained Mary Haines. Evidently the 40 strokes weren't considered exactly a privilege by the brush wielders.

The second complaint came a few days later at approximately two minutes after nine in the evening. Mary Haines and Henny had long since been put to bed. William was outlining the next day's class lectures in the study. In the kitchen Aunt Prue hummed "Over Jordan" as she mixed the bread sponge. In the parlor Miss Sarah perused the latest *Godey's Lady's Book* and then the grandfather clock in the dining room struck nine. Almost before the last bong ceased to vibrate, Miss Sarah's precise step could be heard on the stair. Seconds later, a prolonged shriek came from the direction of the upstairs guest room.

William rushed from the study to the stairs and took them three at a bound. Aunt Prue puffed after him.

Beside the open guest room door stood Miss Sarah pointing an accusing finger at something within. "Look what those dreadful children have done!" She clutched the doorframe for support. "Do bring the smelling salts, Prue. I'm most overcome. I—I truly thought there was a man in my bed! Imagine, a man in my bed!"

Following the direction the finger pointed, William saw pillowed in Miss Sarah's bed the plaster of Paris bust of himself (a Cincinnati sculptor had made the likeness) wearing his own nightcap.

"You must chastise those children soundly, Professor. To think they would do such a thing after all I've done for them. Tsk! Tsk! What are children coming to? No respect . . ."

"If you will hand me the bust," William interrupted, "I will take the offensive thing away." Then consoling Miss Sarah with a promise to deal with the culprits in the morning, he tucked the bust under his arm and went back downstairs to his study.

Aunt Prue followed and stopped at the study door. "Marsa McGuffey, don't you be too hard on them chillun. That Miz Sarah woman . . ." Aunt Prue shook her head. "All the livelong day it's don't do this, don't do that."

"I won't be too hard," William promised. He closed the door, placed the bust on his study desk, and sat staring at it. He couldn't resist a chuckle. Instead of the plaster figure before him, he saw a rattrap that had been placed in a hired man's bed some 20 years before. "Like father, like daughter," he said aloud.

The prank would have made an excellent reader story but it never achieved that status. William's sympathy was too much on the side of the pranksters to add the proper moral. Nor did the bust gain the desired end for Mary Haines and Henny as the rattrap had for their father. Miss Sarah did not make her exit until Harriet came home, and then it was a hasty one. The incident resulted in one of the few instances when gentle Harriet took William to task.

The *First Reader* was complete. It featured 55 lessons with an unheard-of 153 pictures. True, some of the pictures hinted of old-world customs, a cricket bat, thatched English cottages, and boys wearing round-about jackets with wide ruffled collars, but they were pictures nevertheless, and the stories were definitely New World . . . new-West. William offered a student, Benjamin Chidlaw, five dollars to make a copy of the manuscript. Benjamin had walked five days from his log cabin home in Delaware County to attend Miami, and to stretch his finances, he was cooking his own meals at 32 cents a week on a dormitory stove. He was pleased to get the work. Soon both the original and the copy of the *First Reader* lay on William's desk.

William believed in the reader. He knew it was good. But no matter how good, of what use was a reader still in manuscript form lying on the author's desk. He had no available funds to publish the little book himself and no publisher interested in a book for children. However, he went ahead with the *Second Reader*.

Was it coincidence or did providence have a hand in the unsolicited letter received soon after? Winthrop B. Smith of Truman and Smith, Cincinnati publishers, wrote that their firm was interested in publishing a series of eclectic (selective materials from various sources) readers slanted toward the rural West. The writer had been advised of Professor McGuffey's unusual training school. Would he be interested in a contract?

The correspondence resulted in William signing a contract to submit a primer, four readers, and a speller for the net sum of $1,000 to be paid in royalties at 10 percent. And so it came about that during the summer of 1836, readers one and two dried their ink and tried their fledgling wings for the coming reader contest. Many eastern publishers had suddenly become aware of the great reader market in the West and began pushing anything that simulated a reader. How the McGuffey Eclectic Readers would fare remained to be seen.

In the meantime William became involved in other problems, problems triggered by the saloons which he had deplored since the day he and Alec first rode down the main street of Oxford. The year 1835 to 1836 had proved an especially trying year. Eleven students had been expelled for drunken rioting or disorderly conduct. During one melee, a Southern student had discharged a pistol; in another, a Northern student had attacked with cowhide and dirk.

In vain President Bishop appealed to saloon keepers to refuse liquor to students. He threatened to expose grocers who had ruined both old and young by luring them to buy hard liquor. The trustees appealed to the Ohio legislature to ban saloons in Oxford, because it was a university town, all to no avail.

William's principles of rugged Calvinistic discipline flared, became acute, and demanded action. He believed that, "Those vines which flourish most, need the most pruning." He also believed that a family, school family or home family, should wash its own soiled homespun, not ask someone else to do it. He launched a campaign among faculty members for a clamp-down in discipline. At first, the entire staff, except for President Bishop, agreed with him. Bishop was a kindly, indulgent "Eli" in both his own and the school family. He held out for self-government.

Self-government might work in Edinburgh, where President Bishop had trained, and in old established communities, William argued, but the students who came to Miami, some of them only 14, were for the most part naive boys who had grown up as had he in the backwoods. Like trees transplanted from the forest, they needed the protection of a strong fence until they became established, a fence of disciplinary restrictions. "Under the present laxity," he insisted, "they are more apt to become drunkards and gamblers than good scholars."

The professor of science, turning on his first vote, spearheaded an opposition. Of the resulting faculty split, the professor of mathematics who resigned later wrote to William: "All of your labor to maintain discipline would have been of no avail while surrounded by those who, to my certain knowledge, use the most disingenious arts to undermine your efforts and blacken your character."

William knew the only course left for him was to resign. His last months at the university buried in the wilderness had been as rough as the first had been smooth. He tendered his resignation on August 26, 1836. It was accepted without comment.

CHAPTER NINE

President in Queen City

The same month that William resigned as chair of Mental and Moral Philosophy at Miami University (August 1836) brought him three invitations from widely separated educational institutions to join their staffs. The first was from a southern college, and William crossed the Ohio to investigate its possibilities. On his return he found the second invitation awaiting him. Daniel Drake, prominent doctor and citizen of Cincinnati, "Queen City of the West," wrote that Cincinnati College was to be revived with a most outstanding faculty.

"By the unanimous vote of the Board of Trustees," penned the doctor, "you were yesterday elected President of the Cincinnati College with a salary of 1500 per annum . . . It may not be improper to add that a Normal School for the education of teachers is expected to constitute an important and interesting feature."

The third invitation came from his old friend, Andrew Wylie, now president of Indiana University at Bloomington, Indiana, urging him to accept the professorship of Mental and Moral Philosophy at Indiana University, ". . . rather than some southern college. Professor Elliot joins me heart, head, and hair in the above. Come and be happy and free . . ."

William's heart pulled for Bloomington but his head dictated Cincinnati. In addition to the outstanding staff, the Normal School interested him tremendously. Also, in Cincinnati he would be in contact with the publishers of his school readers. There, too, the Institute of College Teachers, of which he was a charter member, met regularly, and he would have the opportunity to "speak out" in behalf of common schools, teacher training, and the need of a state superintendent of schools. And last, but very important to William, there Alec—now graduated from Washington College—would again join the family. He was now teaching *Belles-Lettres* at Woodward College in Cincinnati while attending law school. William sharpened a quill and wrote:

"Board of Trustees of Cincinnati College
Gentlemen,
To your official communication announcing my election to the presidency of Cincinnati College and a professorship in the same I beg leave to reply—that I accept the appointments and am ready to enter upon my official duties as early as may be desirable.
I remain gentlemen, with due respect and esteem, yours
Wm. H. McGuffey"

In the hush of early morning a wagon loaded with the McGuffey furniture—the octagonal table, being cumbersome and its major role accomplished, was left behind—rumbled away from the red brick house on Spring Street toward Cincinnati. The family would follow in the buggy pulled by old Charley. Holding his 6-month-old son, William stood at the horse's head. The little girls, impatient to be on the way, were already in the buggy. Harriet had gone back into the house to see that nothing had been left that should go. William knew her real reason was to say good-bye to the home they had planned and built with carefully hoarded funds; the home she would have been happy and content to live in the rest of her life; the home that had now been leased to a stranger. William estimated the growth of the maple beside the gate. Even he felt a traitorous twinge.

Harriet closed the door of the sunny east veranda behind her, glanced at the logs under the elms where the training school had convened on warm days, paused at the oleanders beside the front portico, and then walked briskly toward the waiting buggy. William's mind leaped to Ruth's statement to her mother-in-law, Naomi: "Whither thou goest I will go." Harriet was the embodiment of the scripture's deepest meaning.

Good-byes were exchanged with friends who had come to say a last farewell in spite of the early hour. William helped Harriet into the carriage, handed baby Charles to her, climbed in himself, and took Henny on his knee. Mary Haines sat on the seat between them. He unwound the reins from the ship stock and clucked to old Charley. The buggy began to move in the direction the wagon had taken.

When finally the caravan halted in front of a rented red brick house on Western Row in Cincinnati, Alec, now 20, and as tall as William but more slender, was there to welcome them. Fastidious in dress, he wore checkered trousers, the newest vogue, and was obviously taken aback when Henny greeted him with, "Who gave you the tablecloth, Uncle Alec, to make your pants?"

Again the hanging of Harriet's portrait over the mantel initiated a new home. Scarcely had the last tack been driven into the ingrain carpet when publisher Smith sent for the author of the readers.

William climbed the stairs to the second floor at 150 Main Street. The tall narrow structure was five stories high and five windows wide. Lettering on the door read, "Truman and Smith, Publishers."

Mr. Smith shook hands. "Welcome to Cincinnati. Your coming spells convenience for us." Then taking a small book from a shelf of identical books, he held it out to William. "With the publishers' compliments, the premier copy of *The Eclectic First Reader*."

William's hand trembled a bit as he took the little volume, the covers of which held captive a portion of the crystallized experiences of home school, log school, and training school. Bound with brown cardboard and backed with black cloth, the reader measured approximately four by six inches. At the top of a filigree-bordered rectangle almost cover size, bold type proclaimed THE ECLECTIC FIRST READER. Centered below the title, a line drawing pictured a mother with young son and daughter enjoying a book in the shade of trees. Beneath the picture, small print announced the reader's authorship, "by Wm. H. McGuffey, Professor in Miami University, Oxford."

After a pleasant hour with Mr. Smith in which the publisher spoke of his high hopes for the series, William hurried home with the little book. Mary Haines and Henny should be the first to own a McGuffey reader.

A book of their very own. And just their size. Excitedly, the little girls turned page after page making discoveries. Meeting the story children and story animals in picture and print was like meeting former friends of the Knuckle Whistle School.

With ease William adjusted to his new position as head of Cincinnati College and of its philosophy department. A classroom lectern or church pulpit never failed to make him feel at home whether the building be log cabin or a palatial design. Cincinnati College, the most beautiful edifice in Ohio, ranked with the palatial. Its curriculum was patterned after German universities with faculties of medicine, law, and liberal arts. Financed by yearly endowments of wealthy citizens, and staffed with professors who had already earned the appellation "genius," its future seemed secure.

Cincinnati, educational center of the West, contributed a colorful environment. With streets curving around progressively higher green hills, like rows of seats in an outdoor arena, it presented a daily pageant of boats on the Ohio, which flowed a third-of-a-mile wide past the college's front door. It offered a mixture of urban and rural cultures. Oratory vied with riverfront jargon, medicine with superstition, fringed surreys with handcarts. Well-to-do citizens thought nothing of keeping cows. The animals grazed in a common herd on the heights during the day, and at milking time they filed down the unpaved streets to waiting tubs of mash, each plodding toward their respective owners' homes.

The homecoming of the cows became a guessing game for the McGuffey children. Which cow would come home first—the red, black, or brindle one, the one with horns or the one with a bobbed tail? But better than guessing about cows, or watching boats on the river, they liked running errands to the grocery on the corner of their block. The grocer, to them the kindest man in Cincinnati, maybe in the world, handed out sticks of peppermint or horehound, and sometimes all the lemon drops a cupped fist could hold. Ill-fated was the day their father forbade them to accept any more candy from the grocer. They complained to their mother.

"Your father has spoken," was all the explanation she deemed necessary. Not until years afterward did they learn that the grocer had charged their father for every stick of candy and every lemon drop that he "gave" them.

As soon as the family and college resolved themselves into a settled routine, William, with Harriet's and Alec's help, set to work completing his contract with Truman and Smith. No "knuckle whistle school" was needed to compile the more advanced readers. If Harriet required further experimentation with stories for the almost completed primer, she had two more-than-willing volunteers at any hour of the day. Alec resumed work on the speller, and William often discussed with his literary brother the merit of one piece versus another.

For a time each evening, William closed the door of his mind on collegiate instruction. In memory he opened the familiar door of the one-room school, taught reading, and planned Friday afternoon programs. So transposed, he worked on the third and fourth readers, more formal in content and larger in size than the first and second. Aware that these readers, together with the Bible, would constitute the complete library in many a frontier home, he chose and discarded, chose and discarded, narrowing the titles down to the best available in prose and poetry. Among the titles selected for the *Third Reader*: "How Big Was Alexander, Pa, That People Called Him Great?" "The Moss-covered Bucket," "Destruction of Senacherib," "The Generous Russian Peasant," "How a Fly Walks on the Ceiling," "Lazy George Jones," "Touch Not, Taste Not, Handle Not," and more.

The *Fourth Reader* continued with: "Speech of Igan, Chief of the Mingos," "William Tell," "God's First Temples," "The Venomous Worm," "Capturing a Wild Horse," "The Vision of Mirza," "The Celestial City," . . .

Interspersed throughout the books were slogans, sayings, and proverbs; also copious rules on pronunciation and diction. Each book reminded the reader that, "The voice of song is not sweeter than the voice of eloquence." Always as he worked, William kept in mind the *Readers'* ultimate goal—a unified language and a unified code of good citizenship.

All of the books would be published under William's name although Harriet was chief author of the primer, and Alec, the speller. Ethics frowned on a woman's name appearing on the cover of a book (it was considered indelicate and bold), and as yet Alec was unknown.

The year 1837, in spite of a financial depression, brought an educational triumph to Ohio. In March, Samuel Lewis, a recognized educator from the East, was appointed State Commissioner of Common Schools, three months prior to the appointment of Horace Mann as Secretary of the State Board of Education in Massachusetts. Ohioans, especially members of the Institute of College Teachers, were determined that in the field of education their state should rank second to none.

The honorable Mr. Lewis asked the legislature for a man to accompany him on his organizational trip, an educator acquainted with the curriculum of Ohio's one-room schools, who knew their location, and was familiar with the state's roads and trails.

"Only one man fills that order," said a member of the Assembly. "William Holmes McGuffey."

So that summer William traveled hundreds of miles on horseback, guiding Mr. Lewis over the main thoroughfares and backwoods trails of Ohio. Old patrons and scholars welcomed him, and because of him, they passed on their allegiance to the state's new supervisor of schools. Mr. Lewis, in turn, promoted the eclectic readers by McGuffey. The name Eclectic on the reader cover meant little to country folk; the name McGuffey was their guarantee.

One afternoon the horsemen passed a meadow where a herd boy was having difficulty keeping his headstrong cows out of an adjoining cornfield. While bombarding the wayward beasts with clods of dirt, he threatened with a rhymed battle cry which began: "We met a flock of geese that thought to show us fight," and ended in a triumphant, "We routed them, we scouted them, nor lost a single man."

William motioned Lewis to draw rein. Unseen by the youthful elocutionist, they listened as he ran after his herd, shouting over and over again, first in falsetto and then in simulated bass, the four stanzas of Lesson LVIII of the second reader, "Young Soldiers."

Returning to Cincinnati, William found publishers Truman and Smith involved in a lawsuit over the readers. Publishers of the Worcester readers had sued the publishers of the Eclectic readers for piracy. Upon examination it was found that 10 selections in the McGuffey series were identical to those in the

Worcester readers. Because of the limited source of materials to draw from, compilers found it difficult to avoid the use of the same current popular stories and poems.

William agreed to substitute other stories for the offending ones; he had by no means exhausted his file of stories. Truman and Smith, thinking it prudent to follow the biblical injunction, "Agree with thine adversary quickly," offered to settle for $2,000. The offer was accepted.

When William returned the revised readers, Mr. Smith met him with, "The lawsuit has been put underfoot where it belongs."

William opened the second reader to Lesson 86. It now boasted 86 stories instead of the original 85.

Mr. Smith read the title of the added lesson, "Jonah and the Whale."

A twinkle belied William's laconic observation, "As Jonah found—there's always a way out."

Three of the best years of William's life were spent in Cincinnati, 1836 to 1839. He enjoyed the association of scholastic colleagues both on the university staff and in the Institute of College Teachers. He spoke in the city's churches and lectured on education throughout the state. He saw the readers take leave of the press and begin their journey to the one-room schools by way of steamboat, canal barge, freight wagon, and pack train. And on May 8, 1839, a baby son, whom the parents named Edward Mansfield after the illustrious educator on the Cincinnati College staff, joined the family circle, making it complete—two girls and two boys.

The same year saw Alec receive his law degree and marry the charming Elizabeth Drake, daughter of Dr. Daniel Drake. William felt his choice in coming to Cincinnati had been well rewarded, though a change was now imminent.

The financial depression of 1837 had finally caught up with Cincinnati College and choked off its support of endowments.

The institution was not yet well enough established to sustain itself. "All geniuses and no money," quipped Dr. Edward Mansfield, when the trustees voted to close its doors. But before the doors closed, William had received an invitation to head Ohio University at Athens, the oldest university in the state.

Made cautious by his recent experience, William visited Ohio University and carefully scrutinized the institution's financial prospects. It was supported, he found, by taxes from the land grants of two townships that had been set aside by the state's General Assembly when the country was first settled for the support of a university. The statute provided that every 30 years the land, which would increase in value, should be reevaluated and so provide for the needs of a growing university. The first reevaluation was set for 1840, the coming year. The financial outlook appeared sound, even bright. William accepted the invitation.

Regretful farewells accompanied the McGuffeys as they drove east, family and furniture packed in the wagon. Harriet cradled baby Edward in her arms. Mary Haines and Henny played "dolls" in the crowded wagon bed. William held the restless Charles, entertaining him with stories as the wagon crept toward Athens, a village of 1,000 inhabitants on the north bank of the Hocking River.

CHAPTER TEN

A Fence Gives Offense

Ohio University, a four-story brick structure flanked by identical buildings, East Wing and West Wing, occupied a 10-acre green in the center of Athens. Built on an eminence, it overlooked the valley of the Hocking River. The campus had long ago been cleared of forest trees—too well cleared, thought William as he unhitched at the president's cottage on a corner of the green. He would plant trees at the first opportunity.

For the third time Harriet's portrait was hung over the mantel of a new home. Mary Haines held the baby up to see the picture, and he stretched out his arms for the woman in the portrait to take him. "Look, Mama," said Mary Haines, "Eddie knows your picture."

But hardly had the furniture been put in place when baby Edward became sick and died. In a new locale, with no close friends, the tragedy of losing a second son was hardest on Harriet. William plunged into his work which posed a full schedule: the faculty met at 5:00 a.m. to study French, classes began at 6:00, prayers at 7:00 were followed by breakfast and a period of relaxation, and every hour was filled until lights out at 10 o'clock.

Classes were crowded that year, teachers overloaded, facilities inadequate. William told himself that conditions would right themselves after the reevaluation. The faculty could then be enlarged and proper facilities purchased.

Many students had followed William to Ohio University, especially those who planned to be ministers. He taught the entire theological curriculum from exegesis, the critical interpretation of scriptural texts, to homiletics, the art of preaching. One of his pupils had formerly sat under the author of the currently used logic textbook, written by Sir William Hamilton. Said the pupil, "Dr. McGuffey teaches Hamilton better and more easily than Sir William himself."

A local custom that had chafed William since his arrival at Athens displeased him still more as the winter days grew shorter—the custom of villagers pasturing their cows on the college green. The cows used the same paths as faculty and students, and often bedded down in the lee of buildings at night. Mary Haines and Henny adapted their cow-guessing game to the new situation; which cow would be the first up in the morning or after they had lain down during the day? The children might have fun guessing, but William found absolutely no fun in the guessing he had to do on dark winter mornings as he took the path to the college. The path was not all terra firma underfoot. And if not alert, he might trip over a black bovine back that blended into the predawn darkness. A barnyard smell often pervaded classrooms. He vowed that some day he would fence the cows out.

In March, while trees were still dormant, William sponsored a campus improvement campaign. Students volunteered for the job of transplanting trees from the forest to the college green. A double row of elms became the focus of interest. And then a fence was put up to protect the elms.

Shortly after the last rail was nailed into place, a demanding knock resounded on the president's office door. A group of irate townspeople, all talking at once, demanded that the fence be removed. They had always pastured their cows on the campus green and they had no intention of doing otherwise. In vain William told of the embarrassing condition of paths and tried to make them see the improvement, the shade and beauty that trees would bring to the landscape.

The belligerent men argued their point. What was a little cow manure? And hadn't they spent half of their lives grubbing out trees? Trees were enemies to be cut down, not transplanted!

William was adamant. The fence would remain.

From that day on, William became a target for catcalls and sly mud balls of a gang of boys, sons of the offended owners of the cows. If business took him to the sparsely settled outskirts of town, he carried a red leather riding quirt under his coat in case of emergency. One night on his way home from performing a wedding, the rowdies attacked him with splattery clay balls. When a young fellow attempted to block the path, William swung his lantern and felled him. The blow shattered the lantern which was just as well. At the moment, darkness was preferable to light.

If the campus fence brought a storm of protest, the proposed reevaluation brought a cyclone! The men who leased the property refused to pay the added tax, although it raised the college tax no higher than the state tax paid by other townships. William, chairman of the commission for reevaluation, received the brunt of the blast. "As a recipient of unwarranted [harsh treatment]" he wrote Alec, "I can now better interpret Shakespeare's Shylock." Those refusing to pay appealed their case to the state legislature. The affair dragged on for months.

Repercussions of both the fence and the reevaluation were felt inside the university. The sons of lessees and villagers ignited a spirit of rebellion in the classroom. Trustees ruled that rebellious students and petition-signing sympathizers should be dismissed. William, Scottish hackles up, proceeded to enforce the new rule to the letter. The result: all but one of the senior class of 1841 were dismissed. Perhaps he might have been more lenient had he had the opportunity of reading an entry in the diary of a dismissed sympathizer: "Oh to be back in his [McGuffey's] classes. I loved him so."

In spite of difficulties and dismissals, the attendance at Ohio University steadily increased. From 1839 to 1843 the enrollment all but doubled. And proportionately so did the school's need for additional finance and facilities.

William was dumbfounded when the legislature supported the case of the lessees and succeeded in getting the reevaluation clause repealed by the General Assembly. Evidently the politically minded legislators considered votes for themselves before the good of the university. With inadequate funds to meet current needs, let alone for expansion of the college, William resigned. He and Harriet packed their goods and their family into the same wagon that William had driven to Athens, and drove through the gate of the offending fence back toward Cincinnati.

Now the pact, "what's mine is yours," between the eldest and youngest McGuffey brothers reversed in application. Alec threw open the doors of his home to the homeless, jobless William and family. But not for long was William out of work. Cincinnati welcomed the return of the "most popular lecturer and teacher in the western states" and offered him the professorship of languages at Woodward College, a junior college, and now the city's highest educational institution. William accepted. His field of usefulness, he decided, lay in teaching or preaching, not in administrative work.

During this period of low ebb, word from Reverend Bishop of Miami brought by a mutual friend greatly bolstered William's morale. "Tell Dr. McGuffey it is my sincere belief that if he will join the staff of Woodward College and organize a church of his own, that his church will soon be the largest in Cincinnati." William appreciated the counsel, but more than the counsel, he appreciated knowing there was no rift between his and his former Miami president.

Winthrop B. Smith considered Professor McGuffey's return to Cincinnati a great opportunity and quickly asked for an interview. Once again William climbed the stairs at 150 Main Street and opened the familiar door, except now it advertised W. B. Smith, Publisher, instead of Truman and Smith. The men had dissolved partnership.

Before discussing business, Mr. Smith detailed the events of the morning when he and Mr. Truman made the final break. He had come early to the office, he said, and made two sample piles of the firm's output of books. Since Mr. Truman hadn't much faith in school texts, in the one pile he placed the half dozen or so schoolbooks, including the McGuffey readers. In the other stack he put the remaining titles on the firm's list and topped it with all of the cash on hand. Mr. Truman arrived, and Mr. Smith explained that he wanted to dissolve their partnership. He suggested as a solution that Mr. Truman take his choice of the two piles of books. Mr. Truman, Smith told William, had "pounced" on the pile topped by the cash.

During the two years since that morning the eclectic schoolbooks had justified Mr. Smith's faith in them. The readers had reached the sale figure of more than a half million a year. "For the first time in my publishing career, I'm solvent," confided Mr. Smith. "I no longer have to turn down a side street to avoid a creditor."

The publisher then produced a work sheet outlining a program of expansion that he believed would increase sales even more. This included revising and enlarging the first four readers and adding a fifth reader on the college level. He had contracted with Alec, teacher of *Belles-Lettres* some time previous, as

William was no doubt aware. He would pay $500 for the fifth reader, given in three installments after receiving the manuscript. Smith had hired a qualified man to help revise and enlarge the first four readers, and he hoped that William would supervise the entire project, once they had agreed on the financial arrangements. William consented.

The brothers, living in the same house, sandwiched the reader project into their busy routine as a sort of literary recreation and relaxation. Each acted as counselor to the other. William subtracted, transferred, and added pieces. As a bridge to the fifth, the fourth reader was substantially changed. A significant addition, a poem titled "The Hand-Post" told how Harry, one dark night, was groping his way along a country road when suddenly before him he "saw a form of horrid kind."

"In deadly white it upward rose
Of cloak and mantle bare
And held its naked arms across
To catch him by the hair."

Poor Harry's "blood ran cold" until he discovered his ghost was but a "friendly guidepost his wandering feet to guide." Harry then made a resolution that would become every boy's who read it:

"Whatever frightens me again, I'll march right up to it."

The fifth reader continued where the fourth left off with offerings of "elegant extracts in prose and poetry." The selections ran a gamut of contrasts that would test the young elocutionists of the day: "The Description of a Storm" by D'Israeli to "My Mother's Picture" by Cowper; the pathos of the "Burial of Sir John Moore" to Hawthorne's "The Town Pump" . . . the complexity of Shakespeare . . . the simplicity of Mrs. Heman . . . the fervor of Isaiah . . .

The first four readers were published as *McGuffey's New Revised Eclectic Readers*, the name McGuffey taking precedence over Eclectic, the fifth reader as the *Rhetorical Guide* by A. H.

McGuffey. They were bound in buff boards with black leather binding, a sort of deluxe edition.

Circulation soared. Alec received his final payment, William his final royalty. W. B. Smith was now sole owner of the readers, with the reservation that all subsequent revisions should be "subject to the approval of Wm. H. McGuffey so long as he lives."

Friends chided William that he had sold his birthright for a mess of pottage. "Look at the affluent Mr. Smith," they said.

William's answer, always the same, showed no envy. "The publisher has had all the headache of publication and distribution. His goal is business, mine purely educational." Truth was, William had no concern for the dollars the readers produced. Rather, he had every concern for the boys and girls who, with the aid of time, reduced the books to a backless, nameless state, and who dubbed the author "Old Second Reader."

July, 1845, brought William two invitations that made him hesitate in choosing between them. The one offered the chair of Mental and Moral Philosophy at the University of Virginia, the university established by Thomas Jefferson at Charlottesville, Virginia, as the first institution of higher learning to be founded independent of a church. William had followed the progress of the Virginia university with interest for it had opened its doors to students the same year as Miami, suggesting a kind of twin cousin relationship—the classic eastern cousin, the western country cousin. Teacher competency as laid down by the university's founder and adhered to by its Board of Visitors, "no person of secondary ability," gave the call an aspect of honor.

William accepted the position. And then came the second call, an urgent plea for him to fill the pastorate of Dayton's First Presbyterian Church. A number of questions nagged at his thinking and caused him to hesitate. His decision would no doubt settle for all time whether he was a minister first and educator second, or vice versa. How would a rugged Calvinist fit into a nonsectarian school? Could a man who had never and would never own a slave adjust into the social order of a slave state?

Dr. Drake, William's professional mentor, was impatient that he should even think of passing up such an opportunity as Virginia offered; indeed it was not to be thought of for a moment. Alec agreed with Dr. Drake. As to preaching, hadn't it been William's preaching that influenced his receiving the call? (While on business in Cincinnati a member of the university's board had heard William deliver a sermon and was so impressed that he became an ardent supporter of his candidacy.) No doubt his preaching would be in demand in Virginia as it had been in Ohio. Harriet, too, felt he should stand by his acceptance.

So the McGuffeys began to make plans for the distant move to Charlottesville, Virginia. They would dispose of some of their furnishings and leave other pieces with friends or relatives. For the time being, even Harriet's portrait would be left with William's sister, Anna Harris. Since Mary Haines, 15, and Henny, 13, were in their second year at Doctor Beatty's Seminary for Women in Steubenville, Ohio, it was thought best they should finish their studies and follow the family to Virginia when school closed—in the company of a chaperone of course.

Harriet sorted bedding and clothing and William sorted books and letters. He paused over a letter in a bundle dated '39. Had it been six years since the Miami alumni petitioned him to write a text on his courses in mental and moral philosophy? He placed the letter in the "save" pile on his desk. He would yet honor the request.

On a spring day the McGuffeys bade farewell to Cincinnati. To young Charles it was the day! What 10-year-old wouldn't be excited about a trip down the Ohio in a palatial stern-wheeler that hoarsely demanded right-of-way among keelboats, barges, and broad horns? At the end of the river route a stagecoach continued the thrills. With four and sometimes six-in-hand under the whip of the dexterous coachman, the overland stage lurched and swayed its way through valleys where freshly plowed furrows showed deep crimson, and over wave after wave of hazy blue hills. At regular posts the lathered horses were changed for fresh ones that were already harnessed and ready to go.

Harriet did not share her son's excitement. Each station passed meant a station farther away from Steubenville. Should they have left the girls behind? What if they should become seriously ill? Mary Haines was hearty, but Henny was prone to coughs and colds. At a rest stop she first became aware how widely Southern customs might differ from those of the West. Lettering on doors read not only "Men" and "Women" but also "White" and "Colored."

After what seemed an endless number of mountainous hills forested with pine and oak, the stage finally came to a halt in the village of Charlottesville on the Rivanna River. The clear willow-draped stream ran slowly. The people moved slowly, they spoke slowly. Only William seemed to be in a hurry.

The university had sent a cab to meet the new professor and his family, and Charles availed himself of the privilege of riding outside with the driver. Through the early afternoon drowned in siesta, even the birds were silent, both William and Harriet sat tensely alert as the cab carried them toward their future, which awaited them a mile-and-a-half to the west.

CHAPTER ELEVEN

Pavilion Number 9

Thomas Jefferson patterned the Rotunda after the Roman Pantheon. "Its marble pillars and capitals are exact duplicates," explained the faculty chair as he took the McGuffeys on a tour of the University of Virginia, the institution that had lured them east of the Alleghenies.

From the Rotunda's portico, six pillars wide and three deep, the McGuffeys looked southward down on the Lawn, a rectangular stretch of green. Two-story pavilions (faculty homes), each a different example of old-world architecture and separated by one-story dormitories, bordered either side of the Lawn. All were joined by pillared arcade to the Rotunda. No cow paths here! No Slant Walk leading to saloons!

To the west lay the blur of the Blue Ridge Mountains, to the east, rolling hills with here and there prominent bold heights. The faculty chair pointed toward one of the heights, saying, "That is Monticello, Mr. Jefferson's home. When unable to ride his horse down the mountain to superintend the work on the university he observed its progress through a telescope from his porch." The man spoke so realistically of the experience, one felt as if the ex-president's telescope might be turned on him at the moment. But the illusion faded when he added, "Monticello is now in bad repair."

Harriet's interest returned from the distant view to the pavilions bordering the Lawn. She wondered which was Pavilion No. 9. William's contract stated that No. 9 with supervision of the adjacent dormitory would be assigned to him.

The chairman must have read her searching gaze. "Pavilion No. 9, Madam, is the end pavilion in the row to your right. And now, Dr. McGuffey, we shall see where the School of Mental and Moral Philosophy has its headquarters."

Leading the way downstairs to the Rotunda's classrooms their guide opened the door to the oval east room. More than 100 empty seats faced them. Just inside the door on a raised platform stood the lectern lighted by two green-shaded gas jets set well to the front. William stepped up behind the lectern. He visualized a class of young men before him. Gone were any qualms of strangeness. He was at home.

If only Harriet had some magical counterpart of a lectern to help her make the transition from housekeeping in Ohio to housekeeping in Virginia; but experience and tears seemed the only way. She learned she must carry a small basket of keys, and every morning hold a "give-out" session with the servants who were hired from an agency that kept slaves to let. At give-out she must count the eggs, measure the cups of flour, butter, starch, soap—all supplies needed for the day. And then the separate cupboards, the buttery, the bins must be locked. Feeling embarrassed to lock cupboards with the cook looking on, at first she skipped this part of the ritual and couldn't understand why the woman turned away with open disdain. In time, she learned that servants regarded unlocked cupboards a sign of an incompetent house mistress.

Harriet often wondered what Aunt Prue would have said about such customs. The old auntie had always had full run of the McGuffey kitchen, been one of the family. In a tiny velvet-lined box, Harriet cherished a tarnished coin, her share of Aunt Prue's legacy. When the old woman had finally crossed over the Jordan of which she often sang, she had left her savings, 50 cents, to be divided equally among the Spinning children.

During the lonely period of readjustment Harriet found comfort and friendship in the Howard sisters. Dr. Henry Howard, dean of the school of medicine, and his family lived on the same side of the Lawn as the McGuffeys. The two eldest daughters, Anna and Laura, though younger than Harriet, being very plain and very practical, seemed equally her age. It was the Howard sisters who explained how to cope with the plague of little red ants that humid weather brought. It was they who possessed the know-how that helped Harriet over the hurdle of choosing and preparing refreshments for the school of philosophy's annual reception.

But no help was needed to plan the garden of Pavilion No. 9. For once William found too many trees even to his liking. A former tenant had planted a veritable jungle. William grubbed out all of the trees except an ash under which he built Harriet a rustic seat, reminiscent of the one his father had built for his mother under the silver maple at Gravel Hill. He planted grapevines to shade the piazza and laid out a vegetable garden and flower beds.

Since the Virginia university held no 5:00 a.m. faculty meeting, William arose according to habit and took the two-mile walk to Observatory Mountain where Jefferson had erected an observatory. Nothing now remained but the stone foundation and the indestructible view of the Blue Ridge Mountains. Sometimes Charles, who attended Mr. Cox's village school, accompanied him. Often on a weekend father and son made the climb to Monticello. Never was a classroom more conducive to teaching the Old Dominion, the Stamp Act, or the Declaration of Independence. And never did a son have a more competent teacher than the father who could quote chapters of history and who could out climb him most any day.

"In bad repair" proved to be an understatement of the once classic Monticello.

After Jefferson's death, the estate had been sold to an unsuccessful raiser of silkworms who eventually left it in charge of an elderly keeper of goats and hens. Doors sagged opened. The goats wandered in and out. It mattered not to them that the parquet floor was one of the first laid in America, nor that the garden shrubbery on which they browsed might be rare European imports. Nor did it matter to the hens that the carriage in which they found convenient nests once belonged to the Marquis de Lafayette. From Monticello, Charles brought back botany specimens and an extended knowledge of history while William took from it a deeper philosophy on monuments that endure longer than even the most influential people.

When the Rotunda clock struck 9:00 o'clock on a Sunday morning, William, dressed in black broadcloth coat and wearing a white clerical cravat, entered the university lecture hall and mounted the rostrum. It was gratifying to see, week after week, every seat filled with students who voluntarily came to hear his Bible lectures. Wrote a student of that day, "We always resented the substitution of any casual visitor for our own professor."

Mary Haines and Henny joined the family after the Steubenville school let out. And straightway impulsive Mary Haines, now 16 and a graduate, ran head-on against a Southern custom. The McGuffey's butler, William Given, a personable young Negro, yearned to read and write. Mary Haines volunteered to teach him.

"You can't teach him," remonstrated her father. "It's against the law of Virginia." But Mary Haines, more McGuffey than conformist, taught William to read and write.

Her father closed his eyes to the integrated reading class held in the dining room of Pavilion No. 9. He believed everyone should have the privilege of learning to read and write. Shortly after coming east, at the request of Virginia educators, he had toured the state in the interest of common schools. The response had been discouraging. He found Virginia in a far worse plight school-wise than was Ohio years before during his roving teacher days. Plantation grandees sent their offspring to fashionable private schools, and seemed more interested in blooded horses than in the education of the common people.

Five years crept by, years in which Harriet worried because Mary Haines and Henny were not learning to do housework; she worried that Charles might grow up feeling himself above the manual labor that the Spinnings and McGuffeys knew was honorable. Ladies and gentlemen of the South left such work to servants and slaves. Homesick, she bottled up her feelings, kept them hidden from William who found his work at the university so satisfying and the promotion of common schools in the state happily challenging. A vague malaise gradually sapped her strength, finally keeping her in her room. Alarmed, William consulted the university physician who suggested that a change of climate for a few weeks or months might restore her vigor.

Early in May the family saw her off on the hack to Gordonsville where she would take the cars to Huntington, and then the steamboat to Cincinnati. William placed her in the care of a Reverend White who was en route to a General Assembly of the Presbyterian Church at Cincinnati. A letter from the reverend stated a railroad accident had delayed them, but all was well. Anxiously William awaited a letter addressed in Harriet's handwriting. At last a most heartening one arrived, and in the same post one from Alec. Both told of an enjoyable visit in Cincinnati. Alec added that he was personally seeing to Harriet's safe conduct to Woodside Farm at Dayton.

William had just begun making out final examinations when the telegraph-dispatch arrived: "Harriet dangerously ill. Come at once."

The wording was the same as the telegram received some 20 years before. The outcome must not be the same. In nightmarish haste he reckoned students' daily standing—no time for finals—to determine graduation status. Mary Haines and Henny packed his valise. He caught the hack following the route Harriet had taken less than a month before.

By the way Alec gripped his hand at the Cincinnati wharf even before he spoke, William knew the news was encouraging. Harriet, though still quite ill, was improving. She had eaten canned peaches, the first canning of the season, at a tea party. Everyone blamed the peaches for the nausea, the fever, and the pain in her abdomen.

After William's arrival Harriet rapidly gained strength. He wrote the family in Charlottesville that their mother was much improved, and finally, that she would be returning home with him shortly.

But on July 3, 1850, he wrote a letter that back in Pavilion No. 9 the family hardly recognized as their father's handwriting. Charles brought the letter from the post office and handed it to Henny with the awful announcement, "She's dead." Death was ascribed to inflammation of the bowels, now recognized as a ruptured appendix.

As a minister, William had stood at many a graveside and read the final committal: "Earth to earth, ashes to ashes, dust to dust." Now it was his turn to listen while the words were pronounced over his loved one. He remained in Dayton until an Italian marble shaft marked Harriet's grave in Woodland Cemetery, and then he took the long journey home. There he kissed each of his children, and placing a hand on Charles' shoulder said, "Your name was the last word she spoke." They all wept together.

The winter of 1850 to 1851 grudgingly gave way to March. On a rainy day, defying the boredom induced by the drizzle, William hitched his chair purposefully closer to his desk. The time had come to face the future. What did it hold for him and his family? The girls were fast approaching marriageable age. If ever they needed a woman's heart and hand to guide them, 'twas now. And didn't Charles? What would he, an insecure youth of 16, do without his mother? The boy, almost as tall as he, but teenage slim, was studying at "Bremo" in Fluvanna County under a private tutor. He would enter the university next fall with the purpose of becoming a lawyer like his Uncle Alec. In every letter William wrote, he reminded Charles of his mother's training, but memory at 16 was prone to fade.

Putting aside future problems for the moment, William reached for a quill and paper:

"My dear Son,

I am pleased that you take interest in the Debating Society. You ask for topics to debate. Good ones are hard to find. [Then followed, a list of current topics for debate, also suggestions on debating technique.] I will send the dean a $10.00 bill on your account of $3.00 and he will hand you the change. Think often of what your dear mother would have to do in anything you are contemplating. Remember that the way of sneers is often the path of duty . . ."

William reread the letter and realized it reflected his feeling of inadequacy at assuming the role of both father and mother to his son. He folded the missive, slipped it into his pocket, and resumed his former trend of thought. Unaware that the eaves had ceased to drip, deaf to the burst of a mockingbird's song perhaps because its tangle of cadences so matched the tangle of his own thoughts, he tried to chart the future. Gradually the tangled thinking became untangled and rewound itself into an orderly skein. William had made up his mind as to what was best, a step he once thought he could never take. And with the decision came the first semblance of comfort he had felt in the 10 months since Harriet's death.

CHAPTER TWELVE

And Then . . .

The clock on the mantel whirred a raspy warning that it was about to strike. William glanced up from his writing. Eight o'clock. The hour he had asked the girls to come to his study. His fingers tightened on the quill as he wrote a last sentence. Two months had elapsed since he had made the decision he would now reveal to them.

Mary Haines entered the study first and took the low rocker facing him. She straightened her skirts and folded her hands on the small key basket in her lap. William patted his knee, Henny's customary place in a family council. Though almost 19, she still seemed a child to her father. As they talked of this and that, William became increasingly aware of the questioning eyes turned toward him, the one pair brown like his mother Anna's, the other pair gray like Harriet's. They seemed to ask, *Why did you call us to your study? What are you holding back?*

In sermon or debate William never lacked for words. Seldom did he rehearse a speech. This one he had mentally rehearsed again and again. But under the candid gaze of their appraising eyes, he discarded carefully chosen phrases. At last, almost defensively, he spoke.

"I have asked Laura Howard to marry me. She has consented."

The ticking of the clock magnified the sudden silence. Then Henny threw her arms around his neck and burst into tears.

"Why do you weep, my child?"

"Oh, Father, she is so unlike our mother."

William's voice broke as he answered, "My daughter, I never expect to find another like your mother. But your mother appreciated Miss Howard. You, too, will learn to appreciate her, to grow fond of her as I have."

He gave Henny his kerchief. "Come now, we have plans to discuss. As soon as Charles's school is out we shall visit all of our kinfolk in the West.

"Before you marry?" asked Mary Haines.

"Before I marry."

The trip west proved to be a what-has-happened before in the McGuffey story, a synopsis before the beginning of a new chapter. In Cincinnati, reminiscences ranged from the grocer who charged for his gifts of candy to the first printing of the McGuffey readers. Their annual output had now reached the million mark. "Do you realize," asked Alec, "that McGuffey is fast becoming the most common name in the West? Catch is, most people think McGuffey's a book, not a man."

When William called on Mr. Smith, he no longer had to climb to the second floor for the prosperous publishing house occupied all five floors. Mr. Smith discussed a revision with him, including the re-division of the five readers into a set of six, which he hoped to bring out in 1853. William thought the plan a good one and agreed to help.

On a small Kentucky farm down the Ohio, for the first time Mary Haines, Henny, and Charles met their red-headed uncle, Dr. Henry McGuffey, and 10 cousins. And for the first time they heard the story of the sleepwalking cure. "Did you ever prescribe the cure for one of your patients?" Charles asked.

Henry chuckled. "No, that's a cure I figure is worse than the disease. Besides, not every sleepwalker would be lucky enough to have a dog like Curly to rescue him."

The visit to Dayton centered around the marble shaft that marked Harriet's grave. William and Charles tidied the plot. The girls placed a spray of their mother's favorite oleander blooms against the headstone. The haunting question when viewing a family plot, *Who will be next?*, was left unspoken.

Visiting Trumbull County, they found silver-haired 80-year-old Sandy both husky and hearty. It would be difficult to say who enjoyed the recital of his race with the Indian brave most, teller or listeners. They visited all of the aunts (three—Harriet, Margaret, and Nancy—had been added by Sandy's second marriage) and cousins, but made their headquarters with Anna. On her parlor wall hung the portrait of Harriet, the painting that had initiated three McGuffey homes, so lifelike she seemed included in the family circle.

One evening Anna came in from out-of-doors dangling some sort of contraption from a short chain. "William, do you remember this?"

William laughed. "It's the gremlin of a rattrap that once attached a sheet to the tail of a hired man's nightshirt."

"Aye, and brang ye the job of splitting fence rails," added Sandy.

William left his young folk at Anna's with the instruction to meet him at Buffalo, New York, on a certain September day. He retraced the recent journey back to Charlottesville, and there on September 2 married Laura Howard. A bride must have a heart of gold to consent to share her honeymoon with stepchildren. Laura Howard McGuffey was such a bride.

As prearranged, the McGuffeys met at Buffalo. They visited Niagara Falls, crossed the Canadian border and traveled as far east as the fort at Montreal, Quebec. On the return journey, stopping over Sunday in Burlington, Vermont, they attended two church services, and in the evening watched the red disc of sun sink into Lake Champlain.

"There—there she goes!" shouted Charles as the lake swallowed the last arc of fire.

Unaware that tragedy had caught up with them, the family retired early. Shortly after 9:00 p.m., William called them. Charles had become so ill that he had sent for a doctor.

When the boy did not respond to the doctor's treatment, William asked that a second physician be called in for consultation. The consulting physician said the first had prescribed the wrong treatment, which pronouncement made Doctor Number One so angry he seized Number Two by the collar and would have struck him had William not intervened. The first doctor left in a huff. The second swathed Charles from head to foot with mustard plasters. The miserable boy finally fell into an exhausted sleep.

"Chancy will probably awaken feeling better," William said, and sent everyone back to bed. But at 5:00 a.m. he woke them again. Charles was much worse.

Before the sun set that Monday evening, bringing poignant memories of the previous sunset, Charles lay in a closed casket, the cause of death ascribed to Asiatic cholera. Contact with the dread disease, it was thought, must have been made at the fort that the boy had so much enjoyed exploring. Afterward, Mary Haines recalled, he had complained of a headache.

Burlington's college came forward with consolation, and asked permission to assist with the funeral. Students stood at attention forming an aisle to the cemetery. Student pallbearers carried the casket, followed by family and faculty, through the living aisle to the vault where the body would remain until cold weather. It would then be taken to Dayton and buried beside Harriet in the family plot. The question, "Who would be next?" had been answered.

The terrible blow etched deeper the lines of sorrow in William's face. His eyes took on a sadness they would never lose. Quietly, Laura shifted from the role of bride to the role of comforter.

Registration for the university's fall term began soon after the McGuffeys returned home. And a simple request that William asked of his daughters during that week had far-reaching consequences. A prospective student called at Pavilion No. 9 with a letter of introduction just as William was leaving for class. He asked Mary Haines and Henny, who were sewing a new carpet for their room (black leaves on a scarlet background), to entertain the new student until he should be free to interview him. Though they didn't want to leave their task, the girls complied with their father's request and graciously entertained the young man with conversation and tea. Any such thought as marrying the blond registrant, Andrew Dousa Hepburn, would have shocked Henny beyond blushes.

When William returned and relieved the girls of the imposed duty, he saw in young Hepburn only a prospective good student. He, too, would have been perturbed had someone suggested that one day he would address the young man as "My dear Son," and sign himself "Your Father." But such, time would reveal. Each would find a need fulfilled in the other—William, the need of a son, and Andrew, the need of a father.

Just what Andrew Dousa Hepburn thought that registration day when Mary Haines and Henny entertained him with tea is not known. But he found excuse to call back several times that winter. And in the spring, it was he who brought the medical student, William Walker Stewart, to complete a foursome with the McGuffey girls for strolls in the arcade, a foursome that remained for a long time.

CHAPTER THIRTEEN

Highs and Lows

Life in Pavilion No. 9 progressed in orderly routine, with the occasional high or low, under the capable direction of Laura, or Lura, as William affectionately called her. A high was the birth of a little daughter, Anna. A tragic low when the child died two days before her fourth birthday.

The girls' weddings were family highs for they married happily and well. William Stewart, honor graduate, was already a promising Dayton, Ohio, physician when he and Mary Haines married. Andrew Hepburn had already earned the dual titles of Reverend and Professor of English when he and Henny married on the bride's birthday, July 10, 1857. It had been six years since she unwillingly entertained the young registrant with tea. For wedding gifts William and Laura gave each couple a set of solid silver forks and $100 in gold coins. "God bless you, my daughter, my son," was William's parting benediction.

August brought William a professional high. A letter from the Board of Trustees of Miami University informed him he had been elected president of that institution. A second letter, signed by all the members of the faculty and by the prominent citizens of Oxford urging his acceptance, accompanied the official invitation. What greater vote of confidence could a man ask for! But William had long ago decided his work was that of teacher or preacher, not administrator.

During the 1850s the revised readers reached a new per annum high of a million and a half copies. When someone suggested to William that the books would yet make him famous, he smiled and shook his head. He could not visualize a first reader that sold for seven cents, a second for 13 cents, a fifth for 50 cents, forming a halo around the McGuffey name.

In 1861 came the great national low, the Civil War. William now found himself in a delicate situation—a Northern man married to a Southern wife and living in a stronghold of states rights. He had only one recourse—to say nothing. Years ago he had spoken through the readers. What influence, he wondered, might stories such as "The Seven Sticks," in the third reader, and Webster's oration, "Liberty and Union, One and Inseparable," in the fifth have had on western boys wearing Yankee Blue. His concern included the boys who had recently left his classes to don Confederate Gray. He loved them, too. If Charles were living, which uniform would he be wearing? After all, he had been an impressionable lad of 10 when he came to Virginia.

Students of philosophy came to the oval east room to bid their professor farewell. "Good-bye, Dr. McGuffey, we'll see you next term." If courage and optimism could win a war . . . but William knew something these young men in Gray did not know. He knew the courage and optimism of those other young men, the ones in Blue. The conflict was bound to be desperate and long.

Since classes had dwindled to almost nothing, William now had time to consider a letter marked "save" in his files, the request from Miami graduates to write out his lectures on moral and mental philosophy. He began the first of a four-volume hand-written manuscript. He also accepted the pastorate of the Charlottesville Presbyterian church.

Writing hours became fewer as troublous times grew worse. Virginia was the first state to be invaded by the North. In time its valleys were pillaged bare of food and livestock. Life became so grim that even William, in a letter, referred to the invaders as "the enemy." The university was turned into a hospital for soldiers in Gray and prisoners in Blue. William, with Laura, often worked around the clock ministering to the sick. His most unnerving duty was the preaching of funeral sermons for the young men who had sat in his classes. White markers in the University Cemetery multiplied again and again.

William hated war. When compiling the readers he had included lessons on "The Horrors of War" and "The Miseries of War." At the time he considered them strong presentations. But they paled to almost nothing in the reality of Shiloh, Chickamauga, Antietam, and Manassas.

The Christmas of 1863 brought a riffle of high in the midst of the turbulent low. It came as a surprise in a barrel. The Cincinnati publishers succeeded in getting a barrel of hams and other gifts through to the author of the readers. The books had kept Smith's firm solvent when many other publishers had been forced to suspend business. The following Christmas brought a similar barrel. Aunt Prue would have insisted the blessings came by way of the Jordan rather than the Ohio.

When the Union army approached Charlottesville on March 2, 1865, a six-man committee—three townsmen and three university professors, carrying high a cane from which fluttered a white handkerchief—met General Sheridan on the university grounds and asked for sentries to protect the campus. The request was granted. One month and seven days later the firing of a hundred cannon shot at Richmond, Virginia, announced the close of the war. The men in Blue had won.

That summer, the publishers of the readers asked William to make a survey at their expense of conditions in the South. He traveled 2,000 miles through the Carolinas, Georgia, Alabama, and Mississippi. What he saw appalled him: the prostrate South being bled by the rule of carpetbaggers, Northern opportunists who carried all their possessions in a carpetbag and were elected to office by freed servants/slaves. He learned of the unlawful work of the Ku Klux Klan. He viewed blackened ruins that had been courthouses and churches, and former mansions reduced to rubble. A rusting plow standing in a field told a too-familiar story—no draft animals were left to pull it. A farmer who formerly owned blooded horses now drove a team of bony steers hitched to a creaking cart. Acres that had flourished under slave labor had become jungles of brush, the laborers freed from bondage to bewilderment.

In the midst of bitterness and poverty, former students welcomed William as an honored guest into their homes. They had confidence in his judgment, in his philosophy. They arranged for him to speak to their townspeople. Everywhere, William recommended education as the most direct solution to reconstruction, education for all classes of people, education that included hand and heart as well as the mind.

William took the train back home over a roadbed and bridges sadly in need of repair. He journeyed on to Cincinnati where for days he kept an audience of leading citizens spellbound behind closed doors. He told a story as only he could tell it, with remembered conversation and anecdote, a story no northern publisher dare print in full. In fact, Alec cautioned him to beware. Bitterness between the North and South was still rife.

At the close of the final session of his report, the publishers of the readers—Mr. Smith was now a retired member—presented William with a sealed envelope. The content of the envelope would always remain sealed from the public, other than that in addition to the remuneration check for his trip it contained the pledge of a yearly annuity to be paid the author of the readers so long as he should live—"a voluntary recognition of esteem for the man and the continued value of his work."

Gradually students, aged beyond their years, returned to the University of Virginia. With few exceptions all had one purpose in mind, that of building a new South on an involuntary peace. Some came in patched gray uniforms. There was little money. The university was poor; teachers were poor, students were poor. Three years after the war, William wrote the head of the university business office:

"Out of one hundred and six in my classes, thirty-five have not as yet paid their fees, many of them most likely will not be so able at any time—so take $500 off my salary."

Possessed of inherent Southern courtesy, only rarely did a student exhibit in the classroom unpleasant reactions to the frustrations of poverty and bitterness, but occasionally it did happen. One such demonstration occurred, of all places, in the oval east room where decorum was a rigid requirement.

John Sharp Williams, a young student from Mississippi, sat on the front row in William's metaphysics class. During an oral quiz he answered a question incorrectly.

Thinking the youth did not understand the proposition, William reviewed it step by step. "Have I made it clear to you?"

John shrugged. "No, you have not." The customary "Sir" was omitted with obvious intention.

William's face reddened. Once again he patiently detailed the problem. Then with studied tact, said, "I hope it is now clear to you."

John half-turned his back. "No-o-o," he drawled, "it isn't."

The class gasped. William's arm muscles tightened as did those in his jaw. Had he been a few years younger . . . As it was, he glared over spectacle rims at the insolent young fellow. "It's because you're a blockhead, sir, a blockhead."

But Awards Day proved that John was no blockhead, also that his instructor held no grudge. The youth received the coveted McGuffey award for the best logical analysis of a book-length essay. (In after years when asked his opinion of his old metaphysics teacher, the Honorable John Sharp Williams, Senator from Mississippi, replied, "I sat at the feet of Gamaliel.")

Some adjustments after the war, Laura found difficult. She did not object when her husband preached to Negro congregations, nor when he helped them to build a church in Charlottesville. But when Mary Haines came home for a visit and William Given, the butler she had taught to read and write, came to call accompanied by his ex-slave wife Isabella, Laura quietly withdrew to her bedroom. She could not accept the idea of "colored folk" as guests.

The ex-butler was now pastor of a church in Washington, and Isabella taught the new day school for colored children in Charlottesville. As a token of appreciation for Mary Haines, William Given brought a catch of shad from the Potomac. Isabella showed Mary Haines the reader she was using in her school, *McGuffey's Newly Revised Eclectic First Reader*. "I wanted you all should know the children sure do love your papa's book."

When son-in-law Andrew Dousa Hepburn was elected Professor of English on the Miami University staff, and Henrietta ("Henny" seemed too childish for a college professor's wife) was again living in the town of her birth, William took Laura on an extended visit to Oxford. The Hepburns with their children, a boy and a girl, lived in the old west wing of the university. Mary Haines, with her two, also a boy and a girl, came from Dayton for frequent family visits.

Never did a grandfather and grandchildren have a better time. Grandpa knew how to whittle tops out of spools, how to skip stones on Tallawanda Creek, and how to draw funny pictures of a pig with two legs and a duck with four. He could tell interesting stories—animal stories, Indian stories, Bible stories. William might be Calvinistic in the pulpit, rigidly decorous in the classroom, but with children he was an adorable playfellow.

He crossed the college campus and stood at the picket gate of the red brick house on the corner of Spring Street and admired the maple that had grown so symmetrically tall.

A passerby, noting his interest, remarked, "Grand tree, isn't it? We call it the McGuffey Maple after the professor who planted it."

William held out his hand. "I had the pleasure of planting that tree, Sir, more than 35 years ago."

He walked along Slant Walk toward town where he found that saloons still occupied Oxford's main street, as did cows, pigs, and geese. He hired a carriage and took Laura to see the little church on Indian Creek where he had been ordained. He preached in Garrtown and couldn't but wonder what the elders thought of his broadcloth coat.

"A most enjoyable vacation," William wrote of the trip after returning to Pavilion No. 9.

In his seventieth year, 25 years after his first tour of Virginia in the interest of common schools when the response had been feeble, William had the satisfaction of seeing public schools organized under the state leadership of a former pupil, the Honorable W. H. Ruffner. He shook hands with the new superintendent of schools and affirmed, "This is a high day in Virginia history." In his seventy-first year he completed the manuscript for the text on mental and moral philosophy, and sent it to his son-in-law for checking with the hope it might be published under the dual authorship of McGuffey and Hepburn. Also in that year, he received the second invitation to head Miami University. On the last day of January, 1872, he wrote a letter concerning both the book and the invitation. The letter contained a hint that afterward became significant:

"My Dear Son,

I have no ambition to publish [and] I could not perform the duties of president. Though my health is good I discern certain menacing signs that admonish me to retire from all employment.

"Your Father."

But he did not heed the "menacing signs." March 3, a year later, found him lecturing as usual to his 3:00 p.m. class and in the evening commenting on a work of Ruskin's at the Metaphysical Club. On the way home from the lecture, he was seized with a chill. Laura put him to bed with hot sandbags to his feet. The next day she called the university physician who pronounced the illness inflammation of the brain.

The Hepburns and Mary Haines hurried to Charlottesville. Perhaps the stimulus of their coming accounted for the seeming improvement in their father's condition. Mary Haines had to return home because of illness in her family and Hepburn because of his work, but Henrietta stayed on for several weeks. When her father continued to improve, she at last felt she, too, should go. She held his hand in farewell. "Good-bye, dear Papa. I'll write you a long letter about my trip home."

Shortly after Henrietta's departure, the substitute philosophy professor called to report student progress. "The young men are faithfully fulfilling the assignments you outlined for them," he said. "Every day they inquire about your health, and ask when you will return to your classes."

William sighed. "Oh, to speak to the dear young men again." Then in a whisper, "God's will be done." Minutes later he lapsed into unconsciousness.

Mary Haines and Henrietta returned to Charlottesville in response to Laura's telegram. A student met them with horse and carriage. "He's still alive," said the young man, and hurried them into the carriage.

Laura met them at the door and cared for bonnets and wraps while they, hand in hand to lend each other courage, quietly ascended the stairs to their father's room. He appeared to be peacefully sleeping. On the stand beside the bed lay Henrietta's letter unopened. "Dear papa" would never read it. At sunset, the fourth of May, 1873, he died without regaining consciousness.

Mary Haines and Henrietta, with Laura's consent, made preparations for removing their father's body from Virginia to Ohio for burial in the family plot at Dayton. But the university faculty, hearing of the plan, presented an appeal signed by all its members:

"The faculty of the University of Virginia having heard with great concern, that it is contemplated to convey the remains of Dr. McGuffey to another state for burial would earnestly request the family . . . to suffer the field of his longest and most arduous labors to be his final resting place . . . they would respectfully represent that a man of merit so exalted and reputation so extended belong in death as in life to a wider circle than that of the immediate family . . . The Faculty hope that the institution which he did so much to adorn and advance may be permitted to have the honor of guarding his remains as it will always cherish and revere his memory."

Reluctantly the daughters consented. Dr. Witherspoon, university chaplain, conducted the funeral service in the hushed and crepe-draped Rotunda. The chapel quickly filled until no more could enter. The last to arrive stood in the hall and outside on the Rotunda portico. In attendance were educators, students, secessionists, unionists, abolitionists, former slaves—conclusive tribute that William Holmes McGuffey was respected by those of all beliefs and backgrounds.

Interment took place in the university cemetery beside the grave of his daughter Anna. The faculty would wear the black badge of mourning for 30 days; Laura, for the remainder of her life.

Because of the change of burial plans, Alec did not arrive in time for the funeral, but was present for the placing of the memorial shaft. Never, perhaps, did the familiar epitaph on a marble obelisk have more significant meaning: "Blessed are the dead . . . their works do follow them."

Monuments
In Men and Women

Monuments of granite and plaques of bronze have been dedicated to the author of the McGuffey Readers. Educational centers have been named for him. He has been acclaimed one of America's Ten Great Educators, the co-founder of common schools in Ohio and Virginia.

A great preacher, he preached more than 3,000 sermons. His readers sold more than 122 million copies. Next to the Bible, they were the most read books for three-quarters of a century in America's West. They were translated into Spanish and Japanese.

Even the trees he planted grew into memorials. The McGuffey Maple at Miami University lived 100 years. The McGuffey Elms at Ohio University, under which graduates marched at commencement, lived even longer—the last one succumbing to Dutch elm disease in 1964. The McGuffey Ash, one of the finest specimens in Virginia, still lives.

In the 1890s when a ditch-digging project threatened the ash, a determined faculty wife took her knitting and rocking chair and sat for three days on the proposed ditch line until the Board of Visitors halted the project. Thirty years later, when a wild cherry that the superintendent refused to move threatened the ash, professors in the dead of night girded the cherry—so today, the ash keeps a towering vigil in the garden of Pavilion No. 9.

But the greatest monuments to William Holmes McGuffey are not those sculptured in bronze, engraved in stone, or built of brick. They are not the McGuffey Societies that pay him homage, the collections of his books, the replica of his birthplace, or the trees he planted. Nor is it the McGuffey Museum housed in the brick home he built on Spring Street in Oxford. His greatest monuments are the men and women who for 60 years molded America; women and men whose lives had been molded in manners, morals, and good citizenship by the McGuffey Readers.

OTHER EXCITING STORIES
IN THE FAMILY FAVORITES SERIES

'TRANGERS IN THE LAND
Louise A. Vernon
one who refused to convert
uld be imprisioned, and the
dragoons had orders to kill
nyone who tried to escape.
Paperback.

HE SWORD OF DENIS ANWYCK
Maylan Schurch
NEW!
Paperback.

THE GATES SERIES
by Thurman C. Petty, Jr.

SIEGE AT THE GATES
The Story of Sennacherib,
Hezekiah, and Isaiah
Paperback, 160 pages.

THE TEMPLE GATES
The Story of Josiah,
Jedidah, and Judah's Idolatry
Paperback, 144 pages.

FIRE IN THE GATES
The Story of Nebuchadnezzar,
Jeremiah, and Baruch
Paperback, 112 pages.

GATE OF THE GODS
The Story of Daniel, Nebuchadnezzar,
and Loyalty to God
Paperback, 128 pages.

THE OPEN GATES
The Story of Cyrus, Daniel, and Darius
Paperback, 176 pages.

3 WAYS TO SHOP
Call 1-800-765-6955
Visit your local Adventist Book Center®
Order online at AdventistBookCenter.com

REVIEW AND HERALD®
PUBLISHING ASSOCIATION
1861 | www.reviewandherald.com

Price and availability subject to change.

OTHER EXCITING STORIES
IN THE FAMILY FAVORITES SERIE[S]

THESE WATCHED HIM DIE
Leslie Hardinge
They were there that day—
they saw Jesus die. And
these are their stories.
Paperback.

THE SWORD OF DENIS ANWYCK

Maylan Schurch
Paperback.

THE GATES SERIES
by Thurman C. Petty, Jr.

SIEGE AT THE GATES
The Story of Sennacherib,
Hezekiah, and Isaiah
Paperback, 160 pages.

THE TEMPLE GATES
The Story of Josiah,
Jedidah, and Judah's Idolatry
Paperback, 144 pages.

FIRE IN THE GATES
The Story of Nebuchadnezzar,
Jeremiah, and Baruch
Paperback, 112 pages.

GATE OF THE GODS
The Story of Daniel, Nebuchadnezzar,
and Loyalty to God
Paperback, 128 pages.

THE OPEN GATES
The Story of Cyrus, Daniel, and Dariu[s]
Paperback, 176 pages.

REVIEW AND HERALD®
PUBLISHING ASSOCIATION
Since 1861 | www.reviewandherald.com

3 WAYS TO SHOP
Call 1-800-765-6955
Visit your local Adventist Book Center[®]
Order online at AdventistBookCenter.c[om]

Price and availability subject to c[hange]